WORKBOOK
REVISE
AQA GCSE
ENGLISH
LANGUAGE

TARGETING GRADES 6 TO 9

OXFORD
UNIVERSITY PRESS

Great Clarendon Street, Oxford, OX2 6DP, United Kingdom

Oxford University Press is a department of the University of Oxford.

It furthers the University's objective of excellence in research, scholarship, and education by publishing worldwide. Oxford is a registered trade mark of Oxford University Press in the UK and in certain other countries

British Library Cataloguing in Publication Data

Data available

ISBN 978-019-835918-0

10 9 8 7 6 5 4 3

Printed in Italy by L.E.G.O SpA

Acknowledgements

The author and publisher are grateful for permission to reprint extracts from the following copyright material:

Anonymous 'Letter to my Son, who is leaving home', *The Guardian*, 8 Sept 2012, copyright © Guardian News & Media Ltd 2012, reprinted by permission of GNM Ltd. **Sebastian Barry**: *The Temporary Gentleman* (Faber, 2014), copyright © Sebastian Barry 2014, reprinted by permission of Faber & Faber Ltd. **Peter Benchley**: *Jaws* (Pan, 2012), copyright © 1974, renewed 2002 by Benchley IP, LLC, reprinted by permission of Peter Benchley IP, LLC, via Drinker, Biddle & Reath LLP. Peter Benchley® is a registered US trademark. **Bill Bryson**: *The Lost Continent: travels in small town America* (Secker & Warburg, 1989), copyright © Bill Bryson 1989, reprinted by permission of The Random House Group Ltd. **Steve Connor**: 'Forty Years since the first picture of earth from space', *The Independent*, 10 January 2009, copyright © The Independent 2013, reprinted by permission of Independent Print Ltd. **Sophie Curtis**: 'Digital Learning: how technology is reshaping teaching', *Daily Telegraph*, 23 Aug 2014, copyright © Telegraph Media Group Ltd 2014, reprinted by permission of TMG Ltd. **Frank Furedi**: 'Accidents should happen', *Daily Telegraph*, 30 Mar 2001, copyright © Telegraph Media Group Ltd 2001, reprinted by permission of TMG Ltd. **Sally Gardner**: *The Door That Led to Where* (Hot Key, 2015), copyright © Sally Gardner 2015, reprinted by permission of the publishers, Hot Key Books, an imprint of Bonnier Zaffre Ltd. **Alex Hannaford**: 'An audience with Koko the 'talking' gorilla', *Daily Telegraph*, 17 Sept 2011, copyright © Telegraph Media Group Ltd 2011, reprinted by permission of TMG Ltd. **Emma Healey**: *Elizabeth is Missing* (Penguin, 2015), copyright © Emma Healey 2015, reprinted by permission of Penguin Books Ltd. **Nick Hornby**: *Funny Girl* (Penguin, 2014), copyright © Nick Hornby 2014, reprinted by permission of Penguin Books Ltd. **Catherine O'Flynn**: *What Was Lost* (Tindal Street Press, 2008), reprinted by permission of the publishers, Profile Books. **Laline Paull**: *The Bees* (Fourth Estate, 2014), copyright © Laline Paull 2014, reprinted by permission of HarperCollins Publishers Ltd. **James Rice**: *Alice and the Fly* (Hodder & Stoughton, 2015), copyright © James Rice 2015, reprinted by permission of Hodder & Stoughton Ltd. **Rachel Royce**: *The Unlikely Pilgrimage of Harold Fry* (Doubleday, 2012), copyright © Rachel Royce 2012, reprinted by permission of The Random House Group Ltd. **Laurens Van de Post**: 'Nyika Plateau' from *Venture to the Interior* (Chatto 1960), reprinted by permission of The Random House Group Ltd. **Tobias Wolff**: *In Pharoah's Army: Memories of a lost war* (Bloomsbury, 1996), copyright © Tobias Wolff 1996, reprinted by permission of Bloomsbury Publishing Plc.

The author and publisher would like to thank the following for permission to use their photographs:

Cover: © WaterFrame/Alamy Stock Photo

p54 & p66: © British Retail Photography/Alamy; **p73:** FBP/Getty Images; **p77:** © Andrew Fox/Alamy; **p151:** Marcin Szymczak/Shutterstock; **p152:** NASA.

Although we have made every effort to trace and contact all copyright holders before publication this has not been possible in all cases. If notified, the publisher will rectify any errors or omissions at the earliest opportunity.

Contents

AQA GCSE English Language specification overview

The exam papers

The grade you receive at the end of your AQA GCSE English Language course is entirely based on your performance in two exam papers. The following provides a summary of these two exam papers:

Exam paper	Reading and Writing questions and marks	Assessment Objectives	Timing	Marks (and % of GCSE)
Paper 1: Explorations in creative reading and writing	Section A: Reading Exam text: • One unseen literature fiction text Exam questions and marks: • One short form question (1 x 4 marks) • Two longer form questions (2 x 8 marks) • One extended question (1 x 20 marks)	Reading: • AO1 • AO2 • AO4	1 hour 45 minutes	Reading: 40 marks (25% of GCSE) Writing: 40 marks (25% of GCSE) Paper 1 total: 80 marks (50% of GCSE)
	Section B: Writing Descriptive or narrative writing Exam question and marks: • One extended writing question (24 marks for content, 16 marks for technical accuracy)	Writing: • AO5 • AO6		
Paper 2: Writers' viewpoints and perspectives	Section A: Reading Exam text: • One unseen non-fiction text and one unseen literary non-fiction text Exam questions and marks: • One short form question (1 x 4 marks) • Two longer form questions (1 x 8 marks and 1 x 12 marks) • One extended question (1 x 16 marks)	Reading: • AO1 • AO2 • AO3	1 hour 45 minutes	Reading: 40 marks (25% of GCSE) Writing: 40 marks (25% of GCSE) Paper 2 total: 80 marks (50% of GCSE)
	Section B: Writing Writing to present a viewpoint Exam question and marks: • One extended writing question (24 marks for content, 16 marks for technical accuracy)	Writing: • AO5 • AO6		

How this workbook is structured

Self-evaluations

In order to get the most out of your revision, we would recommend firstly completing the Reading and Writing self-evaluation checklists on pages 6 to 9. These checklists will help you identify strengths and weaknesses so that you, and your teacher, can ensure that your revision is focused and targeted.

Reading

The Reading sections of this workbook take you through the requirements of each question in the two exam papers. As well as guidance and activities, you will also find extracts of sample student responses, marked with commentaries. There are spaces to write your answers into throughout the workbook.

Writing

The Writing sections of this workbook focus on preparing you for the types of writing you will face in the two exam papers. You will also find a range of strategies to help you when approaching the writing tasks as well as practice opportunities.

Sample exam papers

The workbook concludes with two full sample exam papers, one for Paper 1 and one for Paper 2.

What are the main features within this workbook?

Activities and texts

To help you practise your reading responses, you will find activities throughout this workbook all linked to the types of questions you will face in your exams. The source texts also reflect the types of texts you will be reading and responding to in your exams.

Exam tips, Key terms and glossed words

These features help support your understanding of key terms, concepts and more difficult words within a source text. These therefore enable you to concentrate fully on developing your exam response skills.

Progress check

You will find regular formative assessments in the form of 'Progress checks'. These enable you to establish how confident you feel about what you have been learning and help you to identify areas for further practice.

 **Progress check**

Reading skills self-evaluation

Assessing your skills

Use this table to evaluate your reading skills.

First, look back over your work, including any reading tests you have done. Note the types of questions for which you have scored highly and the ones that you have found more difficult.

Then, for each skill identified in the table, decide whether your work reaches the target higher grade skills descriptors or if you are still working at the basic skills level. You should only tick one box in each row.

Paper and question	Skills	Basic skills descriptors	Check ✔	Target higher grade skills descriptors	Check ✔
Paper 1 only					
Paper 1 Question 1	Identify explicit information and ideas	I can identify explicit information and ideas		I can **accurately** identify 4 explicit ideas or pieces of information	
Paper 1 Question 3	Analyse how writers use structure to achieve effects	I can identify structural features and comment on their effects		I can show **detailed and perceptive** understanding when I analyse the effects of a writer's choice of structural features	
Paper 1 Question 4	Evaluate texts critically	I can make comments on a writer's methods and evaluate their success		I can critically evaluate the text in a **detailed** and **perceptive** way	
Paper 2 only					
Paper 2 Question 1	Identify and interpret explicit and implicit information and ideas	I can identify and understand explicit and implicit information and ideas		I can identify and **interpret** explicit and implicit information and ideas	
Paper 2 Question 2	Select and synthesize evidence from two texts	I can identify differences between aspects of two texts, showing some understanding and linking evidence between texts		I can show a **detailed** understanding of differences between aspects of two texts, offering a perceptive understanding and synthesizing evidence	
Paper 2 Question 4	Compare how writers convey their ideas and perspectives across two texts	I can make some comparisons between texts and comment on how methods are used to convey ideas and perspectives		I can make **detailed and perceptive** comparisons and **analyse** how methods are used to convey ideas and perspectives	

Paper and question	Skills	Basic skills descriptors	Check ✔	Target higher grade skills descriptors	Check ✔
Both papers: 1 and 2					
Paper 1 Question 2 and Paper 2 Question 3	Use relevant subject terminology	I can use some subject terminology when writing about language and structure		I can make **sophisticated and accurate** use of subject terminology	
Paper 1 Question 2 and Paper 2 Question 3	Analyse how writers use language to achieve effects	I can identify language features and comment on the effect of a writer's choice of language		I can show **detailed and perceptive** understanding when I **analyse** the effects of the writer's choices of language	
All reading questions except Paper 1 Question 1 and Paper 2 Question 1	Support your ideas with textual references	I can select some appropriate textual detail		I can select and use a **judicious range** of textual details	

 # My target skills

Look back at your completed self-evaluation table. You could check this with your teacher to see if they agree. Now list the skills you need to improve to reach the higher grade skills descriptors.

1 --
  ----

2 --
  ----

3 --
  ----

4 --
  ----

5 --

Writing skills self-evaluation

Assessing your skills

Use this table to evaluate your writing skills.

First, look back over any writing tasks you have done. These should include narrative and descriptive writing tasks and writing to present a viewpoint. Note the types of tasks for which you have scored highly and the ones that you have found more difficult. Remember to use your teacher's comments to help you.

Then, for each skill identified in the table, decide whether your work reaches the target higher grade skills descriptors or if you are still working at the basic skills level. You should only tick one box in each row.

Paper and Assessment Objective	Skills	Basic skills descriptors	Check ✔	Target higher grade skills descriptors	Check ✔
Paper 1 and Paper 2 AO5	Communicate clearly, effectively and imaginatively selecting and adapting tone, style and register for different forms, purposes and audiences	I make a sustained attempt to match register to audience.		The register I use in my writing is **convincing** and **compelling** for audience.	
		I make some sustained attempt to match my writing to purpose.		My writing is assuredly matched to purpose.	
		I can use a variety of vocabulary and some linguistic devices in my writing.		I can use an **extensive** and **ambitious** vocabulary, with sustained crafting of linguistic devices.	
	Organize ideas	I have a variety of relevant ideas in my writing and can make links between them.		My writing is compelling, incorporating a range of convincing and complex ideas.	
	Use structural and grammatical features	I can use paragraphs to organize my writing and sometimes use discourse markers.		I can link paragraphs **fluently** with **integrated** discourse markers.	
		I can use some structural features in my writing.		I can use a **variety** of structural features inventively.	

Paper and Assessment Objective	Skills	Basic skills descriptors	Check ✔	Target higher grade skills descriptors	Check ✔
Paper 1 and Paper 2 AO6	Demarcation and punctuation	I usually write in full sentences and can use full stops and capital letters accurately.		I **consistently** use a **range** of punctuation to demarcate my sentences accurately.	
		I can use some punctuation marks, for example, question marks and speech marks.		I can use a **wide range** of punctuation with a **very high level of accuracy**.	
	Sentence forms and Standard English	I can sometimes use different sentence forms in my writing, for example, rhetorical questions.		I can use a **full range** of sentence forms in my writing to achieve specific effects on the reader.	
		I usually write sentences which are grammatically correct and can use some Standard English.		I can write and **control** sentences with **complex grammatical structures** and **consistently** use Standard English.	
	Spelling and vocabulary	I can spell basic words and some more complex words accurately.		I can spell most words **accurately**, including **more ambitious words**.	
		I can use a variety of vocabulary, including some complex words.		I can use an **extensive** and **ambitious** range of vocabulary.	

 # My target skills

Look back at your completed self-evaluation table. You could check this with your teacher to see if they agree. Now list the skills you need to improve to reach the higher grade skills descriptors.

1 _____

2 _____

3 _____

4 _____

5 _____

Use this self-evaluation to help you to plan your work, so that you spend most of your time targeting the skills that you most need to develop.

Paper 1: Explorations in creative reading and writing

Overview of the exam paper

This exam lasts 1 hour 45 minutes and the exam paper is split into two sections.

- Section A: Reading
  - In this section you will read *one fiction text* from the 20th or 21st century and show your understanding of how the writer uses *narrative and descriptive techniques to capture the interest of the reader.*
  - You will have to answer four questions.
  - This section is worth 40 marks.
- Section B: Writing
  - In this section you will write your own creative text, linked to the theme that appears in the reading section. You will show your *descriptive or narrative* skills in response to a written prompt or picture.
  - This section is worth 40 marks.

How your reading will be marked

Below is a table to remind you of the Assessment Objectives (AOs) that you will be tested on in the Reading section of Paper 1.

Assessment Objective	The reading skills that you need to demonstrate
AO1	Identify and interpret explicit and implicit information and ideas. Select and synthesize evidence from different texts.
AO2	Explain, comment on and analyse how writers use language and structure to achieve effects and influence readers, using relevant subject terminology to support your views.
AO4	Evaluate texts critically and support this with appropriate textual references.

By working through the following chapter, you will practise these skills and learn exactly how and where to demonstrate them in the Paper 1 exam in order to achieve the higher grades.

How your writing will be marked

Your writing will be marked against two Assessment Objectives.

Assessment Objective	The writing skills that you need to demonstrate
AO5 (Content and organization)	Communicate clearly, effectively and imaginatively, selecting and adapting tone, style and register for different forms, purposes and audiences. Organize information and ideas, using structural and grammatical features to support coherence and cohesion of texts.
AO6 (Technical accuracy)	Use a range of vocabulary and sentence structures for clarity, purpose and effect, with accurate spelling and punctuation.

Overall, the writing question in Paper 1 is worth a maximum of 40 marks: 24 marks are available for content and organization (AO5); 16 marks are available for technical accuracy (AO6).

What is content and organization?

To gain good marks for content and organization you need to get your ideas across to the reader clearly and match your writing to whatever purpose, audience and form is required.

You will need to make conscious choices of language and textual features, so that your writing has the intended impact on readers. To assess this, the examiner will look at the way you use individual words and phrases, as well as the way you sequence, link and present your writing. The organization of your whole piece of writing, and of paragraphs and sections within it, will be taken into account.

What is technical accuracy?

Technical accuracy is using words, punctuation and grammar correctly. Your writing needs to show that you can use a range of vocabulary in correctly punctuated sentences, written in Standard English. Accuracy in spelling and punctuation will be taken into account, as well as your control over sentence structure. This doesn't just mean forming sentences correctly, but also means using a variety of sentence structures for different purposes and effects in a controlled way.

Question 1

Identifying explicit information and ideas

This question assesses your ability to identify and retrieve specific information and ideas that have been presented straightforwardly in a specific section of the source text.

Generally, Question 1 does not present most higher-level students with a great deal of challenge. However you need to be aware of the following possible pitfalls:

- This is the first question, so you might be nervous.

- You may think of this question as easy and be tempted to rush it.

- You may ignore the explicit information or ideas the question is asking you to identify as you think this looks too obvious.

- You may not identify the precise focus of the question and select information or ideas related to something else instead.

As you are aiming for a higher grade, you should be able to gain full marks (4) for this question.

Activity 1

Read lines 1–14 of the source text on the facing page and list four things that we learn about Mr Black's office.

A. _____

_____

_____

B. _____

_____

_____

C. _____

_____

_____

D. _____

_____

_____

AJ Flynn left school with only one GCSE. His mother has arranged for him to be interviewed for a job.

The Door That Led to Where by Sally Gardner

'Mr Morton Black will be with you shortly,' said a young man in a shiny suit showing AJ into a large, book-lined room that smelled of hoovered carpets.

5   It possessed an imposing desk with no one behind it or in front of it. AJ was left wondering if it was the desk that was interviewing him instead of Mr Black. It looked more than capable of judging him and finding **brothel creepers** and a teddy-boy shirt wanting. The desk was a dinosaur of a thing bearing not even a computer to make a nod at the modern world, just an inkstand with

10   clawed feet. On the wall behind the desk was an oil painting of a gentleman in a full-bottomed wig that hung in two forlorn curtains, framing a pink, blotchy face. He could almost hear him say in a voice of brass and wind, 'You will never amount to anything, AJ Flynn. Not with one GCSE.'

15   What in all the dog's-dinner days had given his mum the crazy idea of writing to this law firm? He tried and failed to think what she might have said that would make even the cleaner agree to give him a job interview. He wondered if he was meant to sit on one of the chairs in front of the desk.

20   He could imagine it tipping him off the minute he tried, saying, 'I only seat clients. Clients with well-padded bottoms and well-lined pockets.'

Glossary

brothel creepers – a kind of shoe with thick crepe soles popular with 1950s Teddy boys or fans of rock and roll.

⊕ Progress check

Look back at your answer to Activity 1. Use the following checklist to assess your progress.

	Yes	No
Can you find evidence in the source text to prove the truth of each of the points you have made, e.g. identify quotations where this information is explicitly stated?		
Do all the points you have made relate only to Mr Black's office and not any other ideas, such as how AJ Flynn is feeling?		
Did you either include a quotation or **paraphrase** for each point you made?		

Exam tip

When answering Question 1, it is important to make sure that the information you select relates to the specific focus you have been given in the question. Practise this by picking a novel at random from a shelf in the library, open it at any page and make a list of any explicit information you can find linked to a specific character, setting or situation.

Key term

paraphrase: where you express information or an idea from the source text using your own words

Question 2

Using language to achieve effects

This question assesses your ability to analyse the effects of a writer's choices of language. To produce a higher-grade response you will need to:

- show *detailed and perceptive* understanding when you *analyse* the effects of the writer's choices of language

- make *sophisticated and accurate use* of subject terminology appropriately, linking references to language features to the results they produce

- select and use a *judicious range* of textual detail (i.e. quotations and examples) to support your analysis.

You will now explore each of these key skills in turn to help you to build and develop the skills you need to produce a higher-grade response to Question 2.

Activity 1

Look back at the qualities of a higher-grade response to Question 2 listed above, focusing in particular on the words in italics which are the skills that differentiate a higher-level response from a weaker answer.

Using a dictionary, write a clear definition for each of the italicized terms. Remember to think about what this word or phrase means in the context of answering Question 2.

Detailed _____

_____

Perceptive _____

_____

Analyse _____

_____

Sophisticated _____

_____

Judicious range _____

_____

Analysis

The ability to analyse is an important skill if you are to write higher-grade answers on this paper and Question 2 is where it is first tested. Analysing is different from explaining. To analyse how a writer uses language you need to be able to explore the links between writing and its results.

Look at the following sentence taken from a source text. The narrator is a sailor in the Second World War and his ship has been hit by a torpedo. A student has annotated the sentence with some initial notes about the writer's use of language, breaking down the sentence to explore the effects created by specific phrases or language features.

'Holed deep' sounds like a wound. This is linked to 'something vital torn out' which is also physical violence. The use of 'we' identifies him with the ship, as if he had been wounded.

I knew we were holed deep under the waterline, I could more or less feel it in my body, something vital torn out of the ship echoed in the pit of my stomach, some mischief done, deep, deep in some engine room or cargo hold.

The physical reaction to the blow to the ship. It is as if he is physically connected to the ship.

Now look at the extracts from two students' answers to the following question:

'How does the writer use language to describe the experience of being on board a ship struck by a torpedo?'

Student A

This single, long sentence reflects the thoughts that move rapidly through the narrator's mind from the moment he is aware of the torpedo strike. Each clause describes a stage in his understanding. The use of the word 'we' to describe the ship implies that the ship and the crew are one entity and 'holed' is a violent verb that conjures up the image of a human wound. This connection between man and ship is developed further in the second clause, where he feels the blow to the ship as if it were his own body that was hurt. The use of 'more or less' is interesting because it injects an element of uncertainty – he is not sure what he is feeling. In the next clause this connection between the ship and his own body is developed further, where he describes 'something vital' being 'torn'. This is very physical language which we would normally apply to the human body. It is as if he is the ship and the ship is in some way human...

Student B

In this long sentence, the writer describes the narrator's understanding of what has happened. He tells us that the torpedo 'holed' the ship. This is a violent word which is strengthened by the 'deep' that follows. The narrator feels it as if it were a blow to his own body. The violent language continues in the next part of the sentence where he uses the word 'torn' to describe the wound which again he feels in his own stomach...

Exam tip

When you answer this question in the exam, remember to read the source text closely, looking carefully for the following:

- words and phrases chosen for effect
- language features, for example, metaphor, simile
- sentence forms and patterns.

In your response, you will need to comment on and analyse the effects that these words and phrases, language features, and sentence forms and patterns create.

Activity 2

1 Do you think Student A or Student B analyses the sentence most effectively? You should think about:

- the textual details each student identifies and the way the effects these create are explored
- the way textual details are drawn together to develop a coherent analysis of the sentence.

2 Analyse the final clause of the sentence: '... some mischief done, deep, deep in some engine room or cargo hold' and write the next part of the response you felt was most effective.

Detailed and perceptive understanding

To achieve a higher grade in your response to Question 2, you need to demonstrate a detailed and perceptive understanding of the language used in the specified section of the source text, exploring the effects of the writer's choices.

To show *detailed understanding*, you need to take a forensic approach to your analysis of language, exploring the effects of specific words, phrases, language features and sentence forms closely.

To show *perceptive understanding*, you need to look beneath the surface meanings created by specific words, phrases, language features and sentence forms, and develop more insightful comments, as well as considering the combined effects of the language choices.

Activity 3

Now read the following two sentences from the same text about the torpedo strike and look at the annotations one student has made to help them answer the question: **'How does the writer use language to describe the experience of being on board a ship struck by a torpedo?'**

A long sentence, punctuated by commas to give the impression of a series of quick, linked actions and events ☐

'Huge' used to emphasise the ship's size ☐

Alliteration (repeated s) ☐

'Gathered', 'stood' and 'looked', all verbs that imply that Ned was in control but the final passive – 'was wrenched' – tells us that he was at the mercy of the sea ☐

Interesting choice of 'new'. The slope wasn't there before ☐

> The next second the huge ship started to pitch to port, and before I could grab him, Ned Johns went off sliding down the new slope and smashing into the rail, gathered himself, stood up, looked back at me, and then was wrenched across the rail and out of view. I knew we were holed deep under the waterline, I could more or less feel it in my body, something vital torn out of the ship echoed in the pit of my stomach, some mischief done, deep, deep in some engine room or cargo hold.

The physical reaction to the blow to the ship. It is as if he is physically connected to the ship ☐

'Holed deep' sounds like a wound. This is linked to 'something vital torn out' which is also physical violence. The use of 'we' identifies him with the ship, as if he had been wounded ☐

1 Which annotations do you think demonstrate a detailed and perceptive understanding of the language used? Give these annotations a tick.

2 Pick out one annotation that you think does not explore the effects created. Rewrite this annotation so that it shows a detailed and perceptive understanding of the language used.

```
------------------------------------------------------------
------------------------------------------------------------
------------------------------------------------------------
------------------------------------------------------------
```

3 Find one more word, phrase, language feature or sentence form which you think this student has missed. Add your own annotation for this below.

```
------------------------------------------------------------
------------------------------------------------------------
------------------------------------------------------------
------------------------------------------------------------
```

Now read the rest of the source text below.

The next second the huge ship started to pitch to port, and before I could grab him, Ned Johns went off sliding down the new slope and smashing into the rail, gathered himself, stood up, looked back at me, and then was wrenched across the rail
5   and out of view. I knew we were holed deep under the waterline, I could more or less feel it in my body, something vital torn out of the ship echoed in the pit of my stomach, some mischief done, deep, deep in some engine room or cargo hold.

My other helper, Johnny 'Fats' Talbott, a man so lean you could
10   have used him for spare wire, as poor Ned Johns once said, in truth was using me now as a kind of bollard, but that was no good, because the ship seemed to make a delayed reaction to its wound, and shuddered upward, the ship's rail rearing up ten feet in a bizarre and impossible movement, catching poor Johnny
15   completely off guard, since he had been bracing himself against a force from the other direction, and off he went behind me, pulling the trouser leg off my uniform as he did so, sending my precious half-crowns firing in every direction.

Activity 4

Identify and analyse the **extended metaphor** that is used by the writer in this section of the text. Remember your analysis needs to demonstrate detailed and perceptive understanding.

Sophisticated use of subject terminology

Another important quality of a higher-grade answer to Question 2 is the sophisticated and accurate use of subject terminology.

To make sophisticated and accurate use of subject terminology, you need to:

- refer to the specific language features a writer uses as well as exploring the effects these create

- identify and explore more ambitious language features such as **metaphor**, **symbolism** and **sibilance**, as well as more straightforward features such as adjectives, nouns and verbs.

Key terms

Metaphor: the use of a word or phrase to provide an image.

Symbolism: giving symbolic meaning or significance to objects, events or relationships.

Sibilance: a literary device where strongly stressed consonants create a hissing sound.

Activity 5

Look again at the extract from the source text opposite.

1 Find an example of each of the following language features and analyse the effect they have on the reader.

Personification -
- -
- -

Repeated use of participles (-ing) used to denote continuous action - - - - - - - - - - - - - - - -
- -
- -
- -

2 Identify another more ambitious language feature and analyse the effect it creates.

Judicious range of textual detail

To produce a higher-grade response to Question 2, you need to support your ideas with a judicious range of textual detail (i.e. quotations and references to the text).

To use a judicious range of textual detail, you need to:

- choose the shortest and most apt quotation that supports the point you are making

- integrate the selected words into your analysis

- interrogate the quotation by isolating individual words to scrutinize in even more detail.

Activity 6

Look back at your responses to Activities 3, 4 and 5 and use these to answer the following question:

How does the writer use language to describe the experience of being on board a ship struck by a torpedo?

Look again at the source text below and remember to use a judicious range of textual detail in your response.

The next second the huge ship started to pitch to port, and before I could grab him, Ned Johns went off sliding down the new slope and smashing into the rail, gathered himself, stood up, looked back at me, and then was wrenched across the rail
5   and out of view. I knew we were holed deep under the waterline, I could more or less feel it in my body, something vital torn out of the ship echoed in the pit of my stomach, some mischief done, deep, deep in some engine room or cargo hold. My other helper, Johnny 'Fats' Talbott, a man so lean you could have used him
10   for spare wire, as poor Ned Johns once said, in truth was using me now as a kind of bollard, but that was no good, because the ship seemed to make a delayed reaction to its wound, and shuddered upward, the ship's rail rearing up ten feet in a bizarre and impossible movement, catching poor Johnny completely off
15   guard, since he had been bracing himself against a force from the other direction, and off he went behind me, pulling the trouser leg off my uniform as he did so, sending my precious half-crowns firing in every direction.

Activity 7

Read the source text that follows and answer the following example Question 2:

'Look in detail at lines 3–12. How does the writer use language to describe the scene at the South Shore Baths?'

Remember that to produce a higher-grade response you will need to:

- show *detailed* and *perceptive* understanding when you *analyse* the effects of the writer's choices of language

- make *sophisticated* and *accurate* use of subject terminology appropriately, linking references to language features to the results they produce

- select and use a *judicious range* of textual detail (i.e. quotations and examples) to support your analysis.

> She didn't want to be a beauty queen, but as luck would have it, she was about to become one.
>
> There were a few aimless minutes between the parade and the announcement, so friends and family gathered round the girls to offer
> 5   congratulations and crossed fingers. The little groups that formed reminded Barbara of liquorice Catherine wheels: a girl in a sugary bright pink or blue bathing suit at the centre, a swirl of dark brown or black raincoats around the outside. It was a cold, wet July day at the South Shore Baths, and the contestants had mottled, bumpy arms
> 10 and legs. They looked like turkeys hanging in a butcher's window. Only in Blackpool, Barbara thought, could you win a beauty competition looking like this.
>
> Barbara hadn't invited any friends, and her father was refusing to come over and join her, so she was stuck on her own. He was just sat there
> 15 in a deckchair, pretending to read the *Daily Express*. The two of them would have made a tatty, half-eaten Catherine wheel, but even so, she would have appreciated the company. In the end, she went over to him. Leaving the rest of the girls behind made her feel half-naked and awkward, rather than glamorous and poised, and she had to walk past
> 20 a lot of wolf-whistling spectators. When she reached her father's spot at the shallow end, she was probably fiercer than she wanted to be.

Activity 7 *continued*

Progress check

Look back at your answer to Activity 7. Use the following checklist to assess your progress. You could annotate your answer to pick out the evidence that shows each skill.

		Yes	No
Analysing how writers use language to achieve effects and influence readers	I can show **detailed** understanding of the effects of the writer's choices of language.		
	I can show a **perceptive** understanding of the writer's choices of language.		
	I can **analyse** the effects of the writer's choices of language.		
Using relevant subject terminology to support your views	I can make **accurate** use of subject terminology appropriately.		
	I can make **sophisticated** use of subject terminology appropriately.		
Supporting your ideas with appropriate textual references	I can support my ideas with a **judicious** range of textual detail (i.e. quotations and examples.)		

Question 3

Using structure to achieve effects

This question assesses your ability to analyse the effects of a writer's use of structure. To produce a higher-grade response you will need to:

- show *detailed* and *perceptive* understanding when you *analyse* the effects of a writer's choice of structural features
- select and use a *judicious range* of quotations, examples or references to the text
- make *sophisticated* and *accurate* use of subject terminology relating to structural features appropriately.

Look back at the qualities of a higher-grade response to Question 3 listed above, focusing in particular on the words in italics which are the skills that differentiate a higher-level response from a weaker answer.

Remind yourself of the meanings of the key words and phrases that you noted down on page 14.

You will now explore each of these key skills in turn to help you to develop the skills you need to produce a higher-grade response to Question 3. These are the same skills you used in response to Question 2, but you are now applying these to the analysis of structure rather than language.

Analysing structure

The key to achieving the higher grades for this question is to understand the ways in which writers guide their readers through the events and ideas in the text.

In order to show the examiner that you have a sophisticated understanding of this aspect of the writer's craft, you will also need to read like a writer. In this question, though, rather than analysing a text closely at word and sentence level as you did for Question 2, you will be asked to analyse structural features of the whole text. This means looking at:

- the sequence through a passage, for example, scene-setting, introduction of a character, repetition, threads, patterns or motifs
- shifts in ideas and perspectives, for example, movement from big to small, place to place, outside to inside (and vice versa), narrative perspectives
- coherence, for example, connections and links across paragraphs, links within paragraphs, topic sentences.

The examples given in the list above illustrate some of the subject terminology you could use in your answer to this question.

So the key skills that you need to show when you answer this sort of question are:

- *selecting* relevant examples of structural features throughout the passage
- *commenting* on them and *analysing* them.

Read the source text which begins below and continues on the facing page.

The land seemed almost as dark as the water, for there was no moon. All that separated sea from shore was a long, straight stretch of beach – so white that it shone. From a house behind the grass-splotched dunes, lights cast yellow glimmers on the sand. The front door to the house opened, and a man

5 and a woman stepped out onto the wooden porch. They stood for a moment staring at the sea, embraced quickly, and scampered down the few steps onto the sand. The man was drunk, and he stumbled on the bottom step. The woman laughed and took his hand, and together they ran to the beach.

"First a swim," said the woman, "to clear your head."

10 "You go ahead. I'll wait for you here."

The woman rose and walked to where the gentle surf washed over her ankles. The water was colder than the night air, for it was only mid-June. The woman called back, "You're sure you don't want to come?" But there was no answer from the sleeping man. She backed up a few steps, then ran

15 at the water. At first her strides were long and graceful, but then a small wave crashed into her knees. She faltered, regained her footing, and flung herself over the next waist-high wave. The water was only up to her hips, so she stood, pushed the hair out of her eyes, and continued walking until the water covered her shoulders. There she began to swim – with the jerky,

20 head-above-water stroke of the untutored.

A hundred yards offshore, the fish sensed a change in the sea's rhythm. It did not see the woman, nor yet did it smell her. Running within the length of its body were a series of thin canals, filled with mucus and dotted with nerve endings, and these nerves detected vibrations and signalled the brain.

25 The fish turned toward shore. The woman continued to swim away from the beach, stopping now and then to check her position by the lights shining from the house. The tide was slack, so she had not moved up or down the beach. But she was tiring, so she rested for a moment, treading water, and then started for shore.

30 The vibrations were stronger now, and the fish recognized prey. The sweeps of its tail quickened, thrusting the giant body forward with a speed that agitated the tiny phosphorescent animals in the water and caused them to glow, casting a mantle of sparks over the fish.

The fish closed on the woman and hurtled past, a dozen feet to the side

35 and six feet below the surface. The woman felt only a wave of pressure that seemed to lift her up in the water and ease her down again. She stopped swimming and held her breath. Feeling nothing further, she resumed her lurching stroke.

The fish smelled her now, and the vibrations – erratic and sharp – signalled

40 distress. The fish began to circle close to the surface. Its dorsal fin broke water, and its tail, thrashing back and forth, cut the glassy surface with a hiss. A series of tremors shook its body.

For the first time, the woman felt fear, though she did not know why. Adrenaline shot through her trunk and her limbs, generating a tingling heat
45 and urging her to swim faster. She guessed that she was fifty yards from shore. She could see the line of white foam where the waves broke on the beach. She saw the lights in the house, and for a comforting moment she thought she saw someone pass by one of the windows. The fish was about forty feet from the woman, off to the side, when it turned suddenly to the left,
50 dropped entirely below the surface, and, with two quick thrusts of its tail, was upon her.

Activity 1

Decide how you would split the source text you have read into four sections based on when there is a change in focus, for example, a shift in narrative perspective or change of location. Write the first sentence of each section in the boxes below and give each section a title. The first one has been done for you.

Section 1

> **Title** _ _ Setting the scene _
>
> _The land seemed almost as dark as the water, for there was no moon._ _ _ _ _ _ _ _ _ _ _

Section 2

> **Title** _
>
> _

Section 3

> **Title** _
>
> _

Section 4

> **Title** _
>
> _

You may have felt that the extract contains more than four distinct sections or fewer. If so, don't let that worry you; there are different ways to look at the structure of any text. However, it is very important for you to see that the writer has presented the event of the shark attack in a carefully structured way, changing the focus to manipulate the reader.

Building your answer

Consider the following example Question 3 about the source text you have read on pages 24–25.

This text is from the opening of a novel.

How has the writer structured the text to interest you as a reader?

You could write about:

- what the writer focuses your attention on at the beginning

- how and why the writer changes this focus as the extract develops

- any other structural features that interest you.

You will now explore the skills you need to build an answer to this question that will help you to achieve a higher grade.

Detailed and perceptive understanding

To write well about structure, you need to have a clear overview of the way that the extract is constructed as a whole. This should form the opening of your answer, before you go on to analyse the way that it develops.

The overall effect

Question 3 refers to the whole text so you need to consider how the text has been structured to make an impact on the reader.

Activity 2

What overall effect does the writer want to achieve? Tick one word that best sums up the effect of the passage.

The writer wants the reader to feel:

Excitement	
Tension	
Fear	
Sympathy	
Nervousness	

Activity 3

Select any novel from a shelf in the library (or perhaps one of your GCSE English Literature set texts). Open this novel at a random page and read the double-page spread. Work out how the writing has been structured overall and write a two- or three-sentence summary of its structure.

The core structural feature

The core structural feature is the one that all the other features depend on to achieve the overall effect.

Activity 4

Which of the following aspects of the source text on pages 24–25 is its core structural feature?

1. A description of the beach at night	
2. The introduction of a couple of lovers	
3. The description of the shark ready to attack	
4. The focus shifting between the woman and the shark	
5. The fact that the woman is unaware of the shark	

Exam tip

When answering Question 3 in the exam, you need to make sure you don't end up retelling the events of the extract. Make sure that you don't fall into that trap by looking for the core structural feature as you read the passage for the first time, before you answer any questions.

In Activity 4 on page 27 you were asked to identify the core structural feature of the source text from *Jaws*. The correct answer is:

- 4 – this extract is built around the contrasting worlds of the shark and its victim.

The writer shifts the focus from one to the other. Waiting for these two worlds to collide is what creates the tension.

Now read the following openings from two different students' answers to the question:

'How has the writer structured the text to interest you as a reader?'

Student A

This extract starts with a couple of lovers on the beach at night. The beach is 'so white that it shone'. The atmosphere is romantic and carefree – 'The woman laughed and took his hand, and together they ran to the beach', which contrasts with what will happen later. The woman decides that she wants a swim in the sea and she doesn't realise that a shark is out there, ready to attack.

Student B

The extract describes the build-up to a shark attack and the writer has structured it so that the focus shifts backwards and forwards between the contrasting worlds of the shark and its victim. This creates almost unbearable tension as we see the shark, at first sensing and then preparing to attack the victim while she remains completely ignorant until it is too late.

Activity 5

Which do you think is the better answer and why?

A is the better answer because _____

_____

_____

_____

B is the better answer because _____

_____

_____

_____

Supporting your analysis with quotations and examples

You should now write about structure in terms of sections and the transitions between these. Remember the focus of your analysis needs to be on how these affect the reader's response.

Re-read the first section of the source text and think about how it contributes to the effect of the passage.

> The land seemed almost as dark as the water, for there was no moon. All that separated sea from shore was a long, straight stretch of beach – so white that it shone. From a house behind the grass-splotched dunes, lights cast yellow glimmers on the sand. The front door to the house opened, and a man
> 5 and a woman stepped out onto the wooden porch. They stood for a moment staring at the sea, embraced quickly, and scampered down the few steps onto the sand. The man was drunk, and he stumbled on the bottom step. The woman laughed and took his hand, and together they ran to the beach.
>
> "First a swim," said the woman, "to clear your head."
>
> 10 "You go ahead. I'll wait for you here."

Remember, the whole passage is structured around the contrasting worlds of the shark and its victim in order to create tension. Keep this in mind as you complete the following activity.

Activity 6

A student has written a paragraph about this section but has not included any quotations or examples to support the points.

Student C

The passage begins with a description of an idyllic beach scene. The writer creates the image of a perfect summer's night on the beach. This is an attractive, carefree world that almost appears too good to be true, giving the reader a sense that this perfect scene might not last.

1 Select three relevant quotations or examples to support the points made. Note these down below.

1. _____
   _____

2. _____
   _____

3. _____
   _____

Activity 7

1. Rewrite Student C's response on page 29 to include the relevant quotations or examples you have identified.

2. Are there any other points you think should be made about this section of the source text in terms of structure? For instance, what purpose does the dialogue serve? Add a comment on this and any other points you think Student C might have missed. Remember to include relevant quotations or examples.

Now read the next section of the source text. How does the passage develop in terms of structure and effect?

Activity 8

A student has started to annotate this section of the source text, but you should add your own annotations to explore the effects created by the following structural features:

- the narrative perspective, that is, third-person viewpoint
- change in location from beach to sea
- how the writer shifts the reader's viewpoint
- the contrasts created
- the narrative pace of the section, that is, how quickly or slowly the writer takes the reader through the action
- dialogue.

Focus is now on the woman. She's not named – obviously not an important character.

The woman rose and walked to where the gentle surf washed over her ankles. The water was colder than the night air, for it was only mid-June. The woman called back, "You're sure you don't want to come?" But there was no answer from the sleeping man. She backed up a few steps, then ran at the water. At first her strides were long and graceful, but then a small wave crashed into her knees. She faltered, regained her footing, and flung herself over the next waist-high wave. The water was only up to her hips, so she stood, pushed the hair out of her eyes, and continued walking until the water covered her shoulders. There she began to swim – with the jerky, head-above-water stroke of the untutored.

A close-up. Continues the calm atmosphere. This is deceptive – we know what will follow. Adds to tension.

Sophisticated use of subject terminology

In order to write perceptively about the structure of an extract, you need to be able to do the following:

- identify and analyse the effects of a core structural feature (for example, shifting viewpoint)

- identify and analyse the effects of transitions between different sections of the text (for example, moving from description to dialogue)

- support your points with relevant textual detail (quotation or example)

- make sophisticated and accurate use of relevant terminology.

So far, we have looked at the first three bullet points. Before you go on to write a full answer to Question 3, let's turn our attention to the fourth.

When we identify language features (the other part of this Assessment Objective which is assessed in Question 2), we have a number of terms that we can use to describe them, for example, simile, metaphor and so on.

When we write about structure, however, we need to use completely different language. Because structure is about transitions from one feature to another, we are likely to use verbs much more often. So we would write:

> At this point the focus *shifts*...   or

> The writer *slows* the action here in order to…

This is because structural features are the ways in which a writer guides us through the text so we must describe them as actions.

Activity 9

Select two annotations that you made in Activity 8. These annotations must relate to different structural features (for example, narrative perspective and change of location).

Now write a sentence or two about each of your selected annotations, using relevant terminology and quotations or examples.

1. --

Exam tip

Think about how you can use the following list of terms to describe structure when answering Question 3 in the exam.

- The author then *introduces*
- The author *returns to*
- The focus *widens*
- The focus *narrows down*
- The writer *shifts away from*
- The writer *changes the scene to*
- This *contrasts* with
- This *echoes*
- This *emphasizes*
- The pace *increases* (or *slows*)
- The character or scene is *frozen*
- The writer *takes us back* (or *forward*) in time
- The writer then closely *describes*
- The action *pauses*
- The reader *is* then *shown*
- This *creates* tension
- This *contrasts* with
- We *follow* the character as

Activity 9 *continued*

2. ....

....

....

....

....

....

....

....

Constructing a coherent answer

Look again at the example Question 3.

> This text is from the opening of a novel.
>
> How has the writer structured the text to interest you as a reader?
>
> You could write about:
>
> * what the writer focuses your attention on at the beginning
> * how and why the writer changes this focus as the extract develops
> * any other structural features that interest you.

When you write your answer to this question, you need to think about how you will organize your response. The bullet points provide suggestions for what you could include in your answer. These might prompt you to organize your response chronologically, taking your reader through the passage from beginning to end, but you do not always have to work that way.

Some texts will be structured in such a way that you might want to talk about the beginning and the end together (because one echoes the other, for instance). Feel free to organize your response in the way that best helps you to explore the structure of the source text and answer the question you have been asked.

It can be helpful when thinking about structure, to imagine the author standing beside you and physically directing you through the narrative events; one minute leading you by the hand or pointing you in a particular direction, the next dragging you along at a run – or slowing you down – or even stopping you dead.

Exam tip

You might find it useful to use some of the following chronological words and phrases to help structure your answer to Question 3:

* At first
* Now
* Then
* At this point
* Eventually
* Finally
* After this
* At the point where

Activity 10

Re-read the final sections of the source text below. Annotate the extract to explore how the writer has structured the text to interest you as a reader.

This part of the text is very different from the first part. Remember to look for the structural features that the writer uses to increase the tension. Think about:

- the way the writer controls the reader's viewpoint
- the shifts in the narrative perspective, for example, from third-person objective to subjective
- the narrative pace and how this changes
- the climax of the passage
- any other structural features you can identify such as widening or narrowing of focus.

A hundred yards offshore, the fish sensed a change in the sea's rhythm. It did not see the woman, nor yet did it smell her. Running within the length of its body were a series of thin canals, filled with mucus and dotted with nerve endings, and these nerves detected vibrations and signalled the brain. The fish turned toward shore. The woman continued to swim away from the beach, stopping now and then to check her position by the lights shining from the house. The tide was slack, so she had not moved up or down the beach. But she was tiring, so she rested for a moment, treading water, and then started for shore.

The vibrations were stronger now, and the fish recognized prey. The sweeps of its tail quickened, thrusting the giant body forward with a speed that agitated the tiny phosphorescent animals in the water and caused them to glow, casting a mantle of sparks over the fish.

The fish closed on the woman and hurtled past, a dozen feet to the side and six feet below the surface. The woman felt only a

Activity 10 *continued*

wave of pressure that seemed to lift her up in the water and ease her down again. She stopped swimming and held her breath. Feeling nothing further, she resumed her lurching stroke.

The fish smelled her now, and the vibrations – erratic and sharp – signalled distress. The fish began to circle close to the surface. Its dorsal fin broke water, and its tail, thrashing back and forth, cut the glassy surface with a hiss. A series of tremors shook its body.

For the first time, the woman felt fear, though she did not know why. Adrenaline shot through her trunk and her limbs, generating a tingling heat and urging her to swim faster. She guessed that she was fifty yards from shore. She could see the line of white foam where the waves broke on the beach. She saw the lights in the house, and for a comforting moment she thought she saw someone pass by one of the windows. The fish was about forty feet from the woman, off to the side, when it turned suddenly to the left, dropped entirely below the surface, and, with two quick thrusts of its tail, was upon her.

Exam tip

Although Questions 2 and 3 are both worth 8 marks, Question 3 involves re-reading the whole passage and is therefore likely to demand more time. You may find yourself tempted to write too much for Question 3 and not leave yourself enough time to answer Question 4. Practise answering questions under timed conditions to improve the way you manage your time in the exam.

Activity 11

Look back at the annotations you have made in Activities 6–10. You are now going to turn these annotations into a complete answer to the following question.

> This text is from the opening of a novel.
>
> How has the writer structured the text to interest you as a reader?
>
> You could write about:
>
> - what the writer focuses your attention on at the beginning
> - how and why the writer changes this focus as the extract develops
> - any other structural features that interest you.

Remember Question 3 is about the whole text. Re-read the source text which begins on the facing page and then write your answer to the question in the space below and continue on blank paper. In the exam you will be given at least a page and a half to write your response.

The land seemed almost as dark as the water, for there was no moon. All that separated sea from shore was a long, straight stretch of beach – so white that it shone. From a house behind the grass-splotched dunes, lights cast yellow glimmers on the sand. The front door to the house opened, and a man

5 and a woman stepped out onto the wooden porch. They stood for a moment staring at the sea, embraced quickly, and scampered down the few steps onto the sand. The man was drunk, and he stumbled on the bottom step. The woman laughed and took his hand, and together they ran to the beach.

"First a swim," said the woman, "to clear your head."

10 "You go ahead. I'll wait for you here."

The woman rose and walked to where the gentle surf washed over her ankles. The water was colder than the night air, for it was only mid-June. The woman called back, "You're sure you don't want to come?" But there was no answer from the sleeping man. She backed up a few steps, then ran

15 at the water. At first her strides were long and graceful, but then a small wave crashed into her knees. She faltered, regained her footing, and flung herself over the next waist-high wave. The water was only up to her hips, so she stood, pushed the hair out of her eyes, and continued walking until the water covered her shoulders. There she began to swim – with the jerky,

20 head-above-water stroke of the untutored.

A hundred yards offshore, the fish sensed a change in the sea's rhythm. It did not see the woman, nor yet did it smell her. Running within the length of its body were a series of thin canals, filled with mucus and dotted with nerve endings, and these nerves detected vibrations and signalled the brain.

25 The fish turned toward shore. The woman continued to swim away from the beach, stopping now and then to check her position by the lights shining from the house. The tide was slack, so she had not moved up or down the beach. But she was tiring, so she rested for a moment, treading water, and then started for shore.

30 The vibrations were stronger now, and the fish recognized prey. The sweeps of its tail quickened, thrusting the giant body forward with a speed that agitated the tiny phosphorescent animals in the water and caused them to glow, casting a mantle of sparks over the fish.

The fish closed on the woman and hurtled past, a dozen feet to the side

35 and six feet below the surface. The woman felt only a wave of pressure that seemed to lift her up in the water and ease her down again. She stopped swimming and held her breath. Feeling nothing further, she resumed her lurching stroke.

The fish smelled her now, and the vibrations – erratic and sharp – signalled

40 distress. The fish began to circle close to the surface. Its dorsal fin broke water, and its tail, thrashing back and forth, cut the glassy surface with a hiss. A series of tremors shook its body.

For the first time, the woman felt fear, though she did not know why. Adrenaline shot through her trunk and her limbs, generating a tingling heat

45 and urging her to swim faster. She guessed that she was fifty yards from
shore. She could see the line of white foam where the waves broke on the
beach. She saw the lights in the house, and for a comforting moment she
thought she saw someone pass by one of the windows. The fish was about
forty feet from the woman, off to the side, when it turned suddenly to the left,
50 dropped entirely below the surface, and, with two quick thrusts of its tail, was
upon her.

Activity 12

1   Take five minutes to read and annotate the following question and
source text on the facing page.

> How has the writer structured the text to effectively introduce the
> character of the narrator, Greg?
>
> You could write about:
>
> * what the writer focuses your attention on at each stage
> * how the writer introduces information about Greg and the
>   novel's setting
> * any other structural features that interest you.

2   Now spend 10 minutes writing your answer to this question using
the writing space below and continuing on blank paper. Remember
in the exam you will be given at least a page and a half to write
your response.

This passage is from the opening of the novel *Alice and the Fly* by James Rice. Here, we are introduced to Greg, a shy teenager who suffers from arachnophobia (fear of spiders) which he refers to as **Them**. In this extract he is on his way home on the bus.

Alice and the Fly by James Rice

The bus was late tonight. It was raining, that icy winter rain, the kind that stings. Even under the shelter on Green Avenue I got soaked because the wind kept lifting the rain onto me. By the time the bus arrived I was dripping, so numb I couldn't feel myself
5   climbing on board.

It was the older driver again, the one with the moustache. He gave me that smile of his. A hint of a frown. An I-know-all-about-you nod. I dropped the fare into the bowl and he told me I'd be better off buying a weekly pass, cheaper that way. I just tore off my
10   ticket, kept my head down.

The bus was full of the usual uniforms. Yellow visibility jackets, Waitrose name badges. A cleaner slept with her Marigolds on. No one who works in Skipdale actually lives here, they all get the bus back to the Pitt. I hurried up the aisle to my usual seat, a couple
15   of rows from the back. For a few minutes we waited, listening to the click-clack of the indicator. I watched the wet blur of rain on the window – the reflection of the lights, flashing in the puddles on the pavement. Then the engine trembled back to life and the bus pulled off through Skipdale.

20   I got a little shivery today, between those first couple of stops. Thinking now about all those passengers on the bus, it makes me wonder how I do it every night. It's not people so much that bother me. It's **Them**. I heard once that a person is never more than three metres away from one of **Them** at any time, and since
25   then I can't help feeling that the more people there are around, the more there's a chance that one of **Them**'ll be around too. I know that's stupid.

We soon reached the Prancing Horse. Even through the rain I could make out the small crowd huddled under the shelter. The
30   doors hissed open and Man With Ear Hair stumbled through, shaking his umbrella, handing over his change. He took the disabled seat at the front and made full use of its legroom. Woman Who Sneezes was next, squeezing beside a Waitrose employee, her bulk spilling over into the aisle. A couple of old ladies showed
35   their passes, riding back from their day out in the crime-free capital of England. 'It's such a nice town,' they told the driver. 'It's such a nice pub, it was such nice fish.' Their sagging faces were so expressionless I could have reached out and given them a wobble.

And then there was you, all red curls and smiles, stepping up to
40   buy your ticket, and the warmth rose through me like helium to my brain.

Progress check

Now that you have practised the skills needed for a higher-grade response to Question 3, carry out the progress check below. Use three highlighter pens of different colours to highlight sections of your answer to Activity 12 on page 38 to show where you have satisfied each of the criteria for a higher grade.

		Yes	No
Reading paper 1 Q3 **Explaining how writers use structure to achieve effects and influence readers**	I can show **detailed** understanding of the writer's choice of structural features.		
	I can show a **perceptive** understanding of the effects of the writer's choice of structural features.		
	I can **analyse** the effects of the writer's choice of structural features.		
Using relevant subject terminology to support your views	I can make **accurate** use of subject terminology relating to structural features appropriately.		
	I can make **sophisticated** use of subject terminology relating to structural features appropriately.		
Supporting your ideas with appropriate textual references	I can support my ideas with a range of **judicious** examples.		

Question 4

Evaluate texts critically

Question 4 assesses your ability to evaluate the effectiveness of a text. To produce a higher-grade response you will need to:

- evaluate *critically* and *in detail* the effects on the reader
- show *perceptive* understanding of the writer's methods
- select a *judicious range* of textual detail
- develop a *convincing* and *critical* response to the focus of the statement.

Activity 1

Look back at the qualities of a higher-grade response to Question 4 listed above, focusing in particular on the words in italics which are the skills that differentiate a higher-level response from a weaker answer.

Remind yourself of the meanings of the key words and phrases that you noted down on page 14.

Using a dictionary, write a clear definition for the following new italicized terms above. Remember to think about what this word or phrase means in the context of answering Question 4.

Critically _____

_____

In detail _____

_____

Convincing _____

_____

The key to achieving the higher grades in this question is to show a perceptive understanding of the writer's methods and to carry out a detailed evaluation of the effects on the reader and how these have been achieved, backed up by evidence from the text.

So there are three key skills that you need to answer this sort of question:

- understanding and evaluating the effects of a text on a reader
- identifying and evaluating the effectiveness of the writer's methods
- developing a convincing and critical response to the focus of the statement.

Evaluating the effect on the reader

When writers set out to compose a narrative text, they must have clear ideas about what they want to convey in terms of theme, characterization, atmosphere and tone. Their compositional skill lies in how they use a range of methods to create these effects on the reader.

In Question 4 you will be presented with a comment made by a student in response to a section of the source text that they have read. This comment will always refer to the author's intentions or the effect on the reader. In this question you are asked to examine these and evaluate how they have been achieved.

Activity 2

Briefly look again at the opening of *Jaws* on pages 24–25 and tick the statements below that you think best reflect the author's intentions.

To make the reader scared of sharks	
To describe the beach	
To enable the reader to understand that sharks are powerful, beautiful and deadly animals	
To introduce the main characters	
To engage the reader's interest by describing the event that will start the plot	

Activity 3

Re-read the extract from the novel *Alice and the Fly* by James Rice on page 39. Write down what you think the author's intentions were in starting the novel in this way.

Exploring methods

In Question 4 you will be asked to evaluate the text by identifying the methods the writer uses to achieve their intentions and evaluating their effectiveness. In order to do this, you need to consider the different methods available to a writer including:

- description

- characterization

- dialogue

- setting

- structure.

Re-read lines 28–41 from the source text.

> We soon reached the Prancing Horse. Even through the rain I could make out the small crowd huddled under the shelter. The
> 30 doors hissed open and Man With Ear Hair stumbled through, shaking his umbrella, handing over his change. He took the disabled seat at the front and made full use of its legroom. Woman Who Sneezes was next, squeezing beside a Waitrose employee, her bulk spilling over into the aisle. A couple of old ladies showed
> 35 their passes, riding back from their day out in the crime-free capital of England. 'It's such a nice town,' they told the driver. 'It's such a nice pub, it was such nice fish.' Their sagging faces were so expressionless I could have reached out and given them a wobble.
>
> And then there was you, all red curls and smiles, stepping up to
> 40 buy your ticket, and the warmth rose through me like helium to my brain.

Activity 4

On reading this section of the text, a student said,

> The writer makes you understand how unhappy Greg is and how much he hates the people around him but there's hope too.

How far do you agree?

Activity 4 *continued*

Write a sentence or two about how each of the following methods contribute to the writer's intentions that this student has identified.

Method	How it contributes to the writer's intentions as identified by the student's comment
Description (language)	
Characterization	
Dialogue	
Setting	
Structure	

Responding to the focus of the statement

Re-read line 21 to the end of the extract from the novel *Jaws* by Peter Benchley.

A hundred yards offshore, the fish sensed a change in the sea's rhythm. It did not see the woman, nor yet did it smell her. Running within the length of its body were a series of thin canals, filled with mucus and dotted with nerve endings, and these nerves detected vibrations and signalled the brain.
25 The fish turned toward shore. The woman continued to swim away from the beach, stopping now and then to check her position by the lights shining from the house. The tide was slack, so she had not moved up or down the beach. But she was tiring, so she rested for a moment, treading water, and then started for shore.

30 The vibrations were stronger now, and the fish recognized prey. The sweeps of its tail quickened, thrusting the giant body forward with a speed that agitated the tiny phosphorescent animals in the water and caused them to glow, casting a mantle of sparks over the fish.

The fish closed on the woman and hurtled past, a dozen feet to the side
35 and six feet below the surface. The woman felt only a wave of pressure that seemed to lift her up in the water and ease her down again. She stopped swimming and held her breath. Feeling nothing further, she resumed her lurching stroke.

The fish smelled her now, and the vibrations – erratic and sharp – signalled
40 distress. The fish began to circle close to the surface. Its dorsal fin broke water, and its tail, thrashing back and forth, cut the glassy surface with a hiss. A series of tremors shook its body.

For the first time, the woman felt fear, though she did not know why. Adrenaline shot through her trunk and her limbs, generating a tingling heat
45 and urging her to swim faster. She guessed that she was fifty yards from shore. She could see the line of white foam where the waves broke on the beach. She saw the lights in the house, and for a comforting moment she thought she saw someone pass by one of the windows. The fish was about forty feet from the woman, off to the side, when it turned suddenly to the left,
50 dropped entirely below the surface, and, with two quick thrusts of its tail, was upon her.

Exam tip

When answering Question 4 in the exam, you need to read the quotation in the question carefully to identify exactly what it is saying about the writer's intentions or the effect on the reader. This will help you to consider how far you agree with this interpretation and focus your evaluation of the text.

Consider the following example Question 4.

A student, reading this part of the text said:

Although you might think that the shark is the villain in the book, the writer shows you what an impressive and beautiful animal it is. You have to admire it.

To what extent do you agree?

In your response, you should:

- write about your own impressions of the shark as described in the passage
- evaluate how the writer has created these impressions
- support your opinions with quotations from the text.

Before you answer this question, you need to establish exactly what the quoted comment is saying.

Although you might think that the shark is the villain in the book, this passage shows you what an impressive and beautiful animal it is. You have to admire it.

The author understands that we tend to see sharks as evil predators. A book called Jaws is likely to portray sharks in this way.

In fact, the writer surprises the reader by portraying the shark in a different way. It is not seen as evil.

The shark is described like a beautiful killing machine. You may not like it but you are impressed by it. So this student is saying that the writer's intention in this section is to make the shark simply a beautifully perfect killing machine. It is not anthropomorphized. Not evil, just itself.

Activity 5

How do the following methods help the reader to admire the shark rather than regarding it as evil in this section? Make notes using the chart below.

Method	How it contributes to the writer's intentions as identified by the student's comment
Description (language)	
Setting	
Structure	

Here is the opening of Student A's answer to the example Question 4 on page 46.
This shows clear understanding and demonstrates features of a Level 3 response.

Student A

The shark is presented as being skilful – 'A hundred yards offshore, the fish sensed a change in the sea's rhythm.' The fish is able to sense things that humans can't. It is at home in the sea, totally adapted to it. The writer seems to be full of admiration for the shark's body and describes how 'a series of thin canals, filled with mucus and dotted with nerve endings' 'detected vibrations and signalled the brain'. This description helps us to understand what an amazing creature it is, a wonder of nature. The woman, on the other hand, is totally unaware of the shark which makes it seem even cleverer. She has entered its world and she is totally at its mercy.

Student B makes similar points to Student A but the opening of Student B's answer is more detailed and perceptive which demonstrates features of a Level 4 response.

Activity 6

Annotate Student B's response to identify the features that merit a Level 4.
Look for sentences and phrases that are perceptive and add detail.

Student B

In this section of the text, the viewpoint changes away from an omniscient narrator to the shark's point of view. The shark is presented in contrast to the humans; where they are seen as inexperienced, clumsy and foolish (the man is even drunk), the shark is portrayed as being skilful and sensitive – 'A hundred yards offshore, the fish sensed a change in the sea's rhythm. It did not see the woman, nor yet did it smell her.' The use of 'sensed' implies that the shark has a sense which we don't possess, something more useful in the distances of the sea than smell or sight. This contrasts with the woman's inexperienced swimming and ignorance. She is out of her element while the shark is completely at home with 'the sea's rhythm'. It's interesting that at this point, rather than a description of the exterior of the fish, the writer chooses to explain the shark's internal sensory system; how 'a series of thin canals, filled with mucus and dotted with nerve endings' 'detected vibrations and signalled the brain'. This impressive ability is explained to the reader in some detail, creating a scientific tone, as if we are watching a documentary on sharks. The writer wants us to be impressed by its physical capability – so unlike our own bodies.

Developing a convincing and critical response

Many students are able to make perceptive and detailed annotations but find it difficult to draw them all together to form a convincing and critical response.

Student B has made the following notes to help them complete their answer. The student has decided that the contrast between the powerful, skilful shark and the inexperienced, clumsy woman is key to the success of the passage.

- Powerful verbs – 'quickened', 'thrusting'
- Beautiful image – 'casting a mantle of sparks over the fish'
- Reader's viewpoint shifts between shark and woman – 'the fish sensed a change in the sea's rhythm', ' For the first time, the woman felt fear'
- Poetic use of long, rhythmic sentence. Sibilance – 'Its dorsal fin broke water, and its tail, thrashing back and forth, cut the glassy surface with a hiss'. Compare to 'lurching', 'treading water'
- Climax of the novel emphasizes the shark's speed and agility – 'it turned suddenly to the left... and, with two quick thrusts of its tail, was upon her'

In order to develop these ideas into a convincing and critical response, the student needs to do the following:

- relate them to the focus of the question

- expand them into full sentences and link them together

- support each point with relevant textual detail (i.e. quotation or example).

Activity 7

Use Student B's notes to help you write the next paragraph of this student's answer to Question 4.

Activity 8

Read the source text on the next page and answer the example Question 4.

Focus this part of your answer on the second half of the source, from line 13 to the end.

After reading this section of the text, a student said: "This made me think about what it might be like to be old and suffering from dementia. The writer really makes you understand what Maud is experiencing."

To what extent do you agree?

In your response, you should:

- write about your own impressions of Maud's experience

- evaluate how the writer has created these impressions

- support your opinions with quotations from the text.

Write your answer to the question in the space below and continue on blank paper. In the exam you will be given up to four pages to write your response.

This is an extract from the novel *Elizabeth is Missing* by Emma Healey. The narrator Maud is an old lady suffering from **dementia**. In this extract she is being visited by Carla, her carer.

Elizabeth is Missing by Emma Healey

'Have I got enough eggs?'

'Plenty, so you don't have to go out today.'

She picks up the carers' folder, nodding at me, keeping eye contact until I nod back. I feel like I'm at school. There was
5   something in my head a moment ago, a story, but I've lost the thread of it now. Once upon a time, is that how it started? Once upon a time in a deep, dark forest, there lived an old, old woman named Maud. I can't think what the next bit should be. Something about waiting for her daughter to come and visit, perhaps. It's a
10 shame I don't live in a nice little cottage in a dark forest, I could just fancy that. And my granddaughter might bring me food in a basket.

A bang, somewhere in the house, makes my eyes skitter across the sitting room, there's an animal, an animal for wearing outside,
15 lying over the arm of the settee. It's Carla's. She never hangs it up, worried she'll forget it, I expect. I can't help staring at it, sure it will move, scurry away to a corner, or eat me up and take my place. And Katy will have to remark on its big eyes, its big teeth.

'All these tins of peaches!' Carla shouts from the kitchen. Carla the
20 carer. 'Carers' is what they call them. 'You must stop buying food,' she calls again. I can hear the scrape of tins against my Formica worktop. 'You have enough for an army.'

Enough food. You can never have enough. Most of it seems to go missing anyway, and can't be found even after I've bought
25 it. I don't know who's eating it all. My daughter's the same. 'No more cans, Mum,' she says, going through my cupboards at every opportunity. I think she must be feeding someone. Half the stuff disappears home with her, and then she wonders why I need to go shopping again. Anyway, it's not like I have many treats left in life.

Progress check

Now that you have practised the skills needed for a higher-grade response to Question 4, carry out the progress check below. Use three highlighter pens of different colours to highlight passages of your answer to Activity 8 on page 49 to show where you have satisfied each of the criteria for a higher grade.

Reading paper 1 Q4		Yes	No
Evaluating texts critically	I can **evaluate** critically the effects on the reader.		
	I can evaluate the effects on the reader in **detail**.		
	I can show **perceptive** understanding of the writer's methods.		
	I can develop a **convincing** and **critical** response to the focus of the statement.		
Supporting your ideas with appropriate textual references	I can select a judicious **range** of textual detail.		

Overview of the Writing section

The writing section of Paper 1 is worth 40 marks, the same as the reading section. You should expect to spend about 45 minutes on your writing, splitting your writing into three stages:

- planning (5–10 minutes)
- writing (30–35 minutes)
- checking, proofreading and making final improvements (5 minutes).

You will be given a choice of two writing tasks and should only write a response to one of these tasks. You could be presented with one of the following combinations:

- a narrative (story) task and a description task
- two narrative tasks
- two description tasks.

Remember you should only undertake one task.

The tasks will be based on the theme of the text in the reading section but you will not need to use any of the content from it. Your writing will be your own creation based on your imagination and life experiences.

> **Exam tip**
>
> The most important thing to remember about this writing task is that it is less about what you say and more about how you say it. In other words, although your writing obviously needs to include relevant content to address the task, it is your skill as an imaginative, creative writer that will gain you the highest marks.

How your writing will be marked

Your writing will be marked against two Assessment Objectives:

Assessment Objective	The writing skills that you need to demonstrate
AO5 (Content and organization)	Communicate clearly, effectively and imaginatively, selecting and adapting tone, style and register for different forms, purposes and audiences.
	Organize information and ideas, using structural and grammatical features to support coherence and cohesion of texts.
AO6 (Technical accuracy)	Use a range of vocabulary and sentence structures for clarity, purpose and effect, with accurate spelling and punctuation.

Overall, the writing question in Paper 1 is worth a maximum of 40 marks: 24 marks are available for content and organization (AO5); 16 marks are available for technical accuracy (AO6).

The descriptive task

What is description?

Description is a more static, poetic form of writing which aims to paint a picture of a scene or experience in the reader's mind. To produce a higher-grade response to the descriptive task you will need to do the following.

Content

☐ Make sure the **register** you use in your description is convincing and compelling for your audience – for instance, aim to convey emotion through the kind of words and manner of writing used. Think, "how do I want my readers to feel as they read?"

☐ Ensure that your writing is assuredly matched to purpose – for instance, think about the tone you want to create: is this humorous or sad? Remember that although the tone should be consistent, the mood or atmosphere created might change.

☐ Craft your writing, using precise, sophisticated vocabulary and descriptive linguistic devices (such as figurative language to bring your description to life, or reflecting the tone of your writing in the sound of the words that you've chosen).

Organization

☐ Incorporate varied and effective structural features – for instance, moving gradually closer to the focus of your description so that your view changes, or focusing on a specific moment.

☐ Incorporate a range of complex and convincing ideas to make your writing compelling.

☐ Construct fluently linked paragraphs with seamlessly integrated discourse markers.

Technical accuracy

☐ Consistently demarcate your sentences securely and accurately.

☐ Use a wide range of punctuation with a high level of accuracy.

☐ Use a full range of appropriate sentence forms for effect.

☐ Use Standard English consistently and appropriately with secure control of complex grammatical structures.

☐ Achieve a high level of accuracy in spelling, including ambitious vocabulary.

☐ Use extensive and ambitious vocabulary.

Look back at your writing skills self-evaluation on pages 8–9 and tick the skills that you need to prioritize to achieve a higher grade.

Planning your description

The descriptive task in Section B will provide a written prompt, scenario or visual image to act as a stimulus for your writing, so use this to help you to develop your ideas as you plan.

Look at the following example task.

You have been asked to enter a creative writing competition judged by young people.

Write a description suggested by this picture:

In order to write a convincing description based on a picture, you need to 'get inside' the image, experiencing the sights, feelings and even the smells that it evokes.

Activity 1

Using the prompts in the box, make some notes to help you to plan your description.

Content: _

Sensations: _

Colours: _

Atmosphere: _

Sounds: _

Viewpoint: _

Smells: _

Other ideas: _

Look at the following notes Student A has made to help them to plan their description. This has been done quickly because it is only the initial, planning stage, but at this point nothing has been identified which would raise the description to a higher grade.

Student A

Content: Modern shopping centre, crowded – weekend? Sales?

Colours: Bright lighting in shops, white and clean

Sounds: Loud, echoing, recorded music in shops, crying child, teenagers fooling around

Smells: Perfume from the department store, food court

Sensations: Being jostled by the crowd, tired from shopping, frustrated, excited by bargain-hunting, looking forward to spending money

Atmosphere: Unreal (separated from the world and weather), air-conditioned

Viewpoint: Travelling on the escalator, walking through the centre, looking down from the upper floor?

In order to write a convincing higher-level description, Student A will need to express complex and convincing ideas. A straightforward description of the scene is unlikely to do this.

There are many ways to introduce complexity. For instance, you might decide that although the scene looks cheerful on the surface, there are tensions, frustrations and dramas. Or you might focus on different people who are experiencing the shopping centre in very different ways. Remember the ideas you choose need to be convincing in order for the reader to 'believe' your description.

Viewpoint and focus

When you are writing a description, it is important to decide on the viewpoint you are writing from. Is your description written in the first person presenting a single viewpoint or in the third person which allows you to share the thoughts of different characters? Whatever decision you make, you should stick to this as it will make your description much more coherent and easier for your reader to follow.

Student A has added the following notes to their plan, describing two people who are experiencing the shopping centre in a different way.

Student A

A young boy is desperate to spend his birthday money on a new computer game. His mother isn't happy with his choice (too violent). Mother trying to persuade him to choose another game instead.

Activity 2

Add your own notes describing two different characters and viewpoints that will allow you to express complex and convincing ideas in your description.

As you write your description, think about how you can guide your reader through the passage. What do you want to focus their attention on at the beginning? How might this focus change as the description develops? The focus might change when there is a:

- shift in viewpoint (for example, cut from one person's perspective to another's)

- change of location (for example, moving closer in to the scene or switching to another place)

- shift in time (for example, moving forward from day to night).

Instead of a visual image, you might be given a written prompt or scenario as the stimulus for your description. You will still need to demonstrate the same skills in your writing, so when you plan try to visualize your own image in your mind's eye.

Exam tip

Remember that the writing task includes the word 'suggested' (or something similar) which tells you that the image is only a stimulus for your writing. You do not have to describe everything in the image or restrict your writing only to what is in it.

Activity 3

Look at the following written prompts. For each one, note down some words and phrases you might use to describe what you see in response to the prompt.

In a garden, with rain dripping from the leaves, and the petals of flowers falling like...

In a busy market, where the stalls are piled high with vivid tropical fruits and the sun bakes your back...

Driving down a motorway, the grey tarmac rolling past my window...

Writing your response

Once you have planned your writing in response to the stimulus you have been given (a written prompt, scenario or visual image), you need to write your description.

Remember, you can change your ideas as you start to write, so be flexible. You may have a sudden brilliant idea that changes your whole plan.

Tone, style and register

You need to consider the **tone**, **style** and **register** you use in your writing and how appropriate the choices you make are to the purpose, audience and task.

A description that achieves a higher grade will be shaped by the writer's attitude to the scene. This will be reflected in the tone they adopt and the language choices that help to create this.

For example, someone who finds cities noisy and dirty would describe a city scene in a different tone to someone who thinks of them as vibrant and exciting places.

Look at the following notes made by Student B in preparation for writing a description of a scene in a supermarket. She has identified her attitude to the subject she is describing and noted down some words and phrases she wants to use in her description.

Student B

Subject: The local supermarket on a crowded Saturday morning.

Attitude: I hate supermarkets because they are soulless places which simply exploit consumers, persuading them to buy more than they need.

Language choices: This cathedral dedicated to shallow consumerism, crowded with spoiled screaming children. Unhappy parents unable to say no to their obese offspring. Mindless consumerism – people like robots. Shelves stuffed with empty colours – worthless products shouting for attention.

Key terms

Tone: manner of expression that shows the writer's attitude, for example, an apologetic or angry tone.

Style: way of using language.

Register: the kind of words and the manner of writing used; these vary according to the situation and the relationship of the people involved (for example, formal, informal, literary).

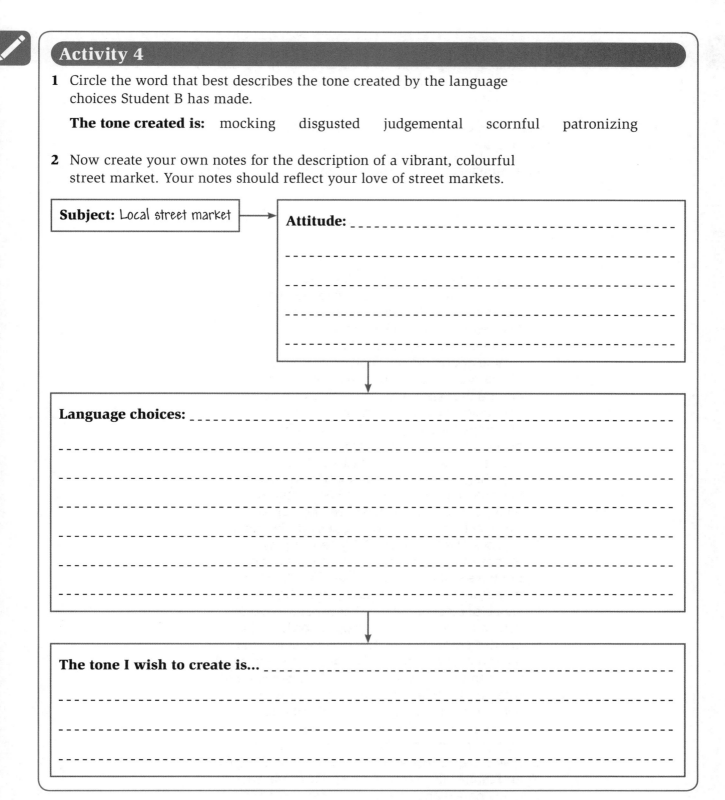

Activity 4

1 Circle the word that best describes the tone created by the language choices Student B has made.

The tone created is: mocking   disgusted   judgemental   scornful   patronizing

2 Now create your own notes for the description of a vibrant, colourful street market. Your notes should reflect your love of street markets.

Subject: Local street market

Attitude: _____

_____

_____

_____

_____

Language choices: _____

_____

_____

_____

_____

_____

_____

The tone I wish to create is... _____

_____

_____

_____

In the extract on the next page the travel writer Bill Bryson writes about his first visit to Las Vegas and adopts a mocking tone towards the place he is writing about. Look at how the highlighted words and phrases help to convey this tone. For example:

'The decor was **supposed** to be like a Roman temple **or something**.'

This implies that it didn't succeed

A very dismissive phrase that implies that the designers didn't have a clear idea about what they were aiming for

Activity 5

1 As you read the extract, annotate the highlighted words and phrases to identify how they create and maintain a humorous and mocking tone.

2 Circle at least one example of each of the following techniques that help to create the mocking tone:

metaphor   **onomatopoeia**   **short sentences**   **precise vocabulary**

> I went to Caesar's Palace. It is set well back from the street, but I was conveyed in on a moving sidewalk, which rather impressed me. Inside the air was thick with unreality. The decor was supposed to be like a Roman temple or something. Statues of Roman gladiators and statesmen were scattered around the place and all the cigarette girls and ladies who gave change were dressed in skimpy togas, even if they were old and overweight, which most of them were, so their thighs wobbled as they walked. It was like watching moving Jell-O. I wandered through halls full of people intent on losing money endlessly, single-mindedly feeding coins into slot machines or watching the clattering dance of a steel ball on a roulette wheel or playing games of blackjack that had no start or finish but were just continuous, like time. It all had a monotonous, yet anxious rhythm. There was no sense of pleasure or fun. I never saw anyone talking to anyone else, except to order a drink or cash some money. The noise was intense – the crank of one-armed bandits, the spinning of thousands of wheels, the din of clattering coins when a machine paid out. A change lady Jell-O'd past and I got $10 worth of quarters from her. I put one in a one-armed bandit – I had never done this before; I'm from Iowa – pulled the handle and watched the wheels spin and thunk into place one by one. There was a tiny pause and then the machine spat six quarters into the pay-out bucket. I was hooked.

Activity 6

Look back at the picture on page 59. Now write a paragraph describing this scene in a mocking tone, similar to Bryson's. An opening sentence for your paragraph is suggested below.

I stood at the top of the escalator and surveyed the scene below.

Vocabulary and linguistic devices

To achieve a higher grade, you need to carefully consider the vocabulary you use in your description. Choose words that communicate the precise meaning that you want to convey. Using a range of linguistic devices will also help you to create deliberate effects to bring your description to life.

Activity 7

Read the following description of a leopard by the traveller Sir Laurens van der Post.

1 As you read, circle effective choices of vocabulary and linguistic devices.

2 Annotate the examples you have identified by commenting on the effects they create.

> We could hardly believe our eyes. A very big male leopard, bronze, his back charged with sunset gold, was walking along the slope above the pool on the far side about fifty yards away. He was walking as if he did not have a fear or care in the world, like an old gentleman with his hands behind his back, taking the evening air in his own private garden. When he was about twelve yards from the pool, he started walking around in circles examining the ground with great attention. Then he settled slowly into the grass, like a destroyer sinking into the sea, bow first and suddenly disappeared from our view. It was rather uncanny. One minute he was magnificently there on the bare slope and the next he was gone from our view.

Activity 8

Write a description of the first sighting of a new species of animal, one previously unknown to science. Use vocabulary precisely and employ a wide range of linguistic devices to create deliberate effects. Continue on blank paper if you need to.

Exam tip

To broaden your vocabulary, learn how to use a thesaurus effectively and adopt new words as you encounter them in your reading. This will help you to make more ambitious choices of vocabulary and employ these correctly when you are writing under exam conditions.

Structuring your description

In Section B of Paper 1 you might be asked to describe a person rather than a place or scene. To gain the higher grades you need to organize your writing effectively, using a variety of structural features for creative effect.

Look at Charles Dickens' description of Bill Sikes from *Oliver Twist*. Here, Dickens structures his writing by taking the reader ever closer to Sikes, using sight, smell and sound to bring the character to life. Towards the end of the extract, Dickens uses Sikes' relationship with his dog to develop our understanding of his character.

Activity 9

1 Highlight the extract to identify where each of the following sections begins and ends. You should use a different colour for each one.

- Sikes' surroundings
- Sikes' relationship with his dog
- Sikes' appearance

Extract from *Oliver Twist* by Charles Dickens

In the obscure parlour of a low public-house, in the filthiest part of Little Saffron Hill; a dark and gloomy den, where a flaring gas-light burnt all day in the winter-time; and where no ray of sun ever shone in the summer: there sat, brooding over a little pewter measure and a small glass, strongly impregnated with the smell of liquor, a man in a velveteen
5 coat, drab shorts, half boots and stockings, who even by that dim light no experienced agent of police would have hesitated to recognise as Mr. William Sikes. At his feet sat a white-coated, red-eyed dog; who occupied himself, alternately, in winking at his master with both eyes at the same time; and in licking a large, fresh cut on one side of his mouth, which appeared to be the result of some recent conflict.

10 "Keep quiet, you warmint! Keep quiet!" said Mr. Sikes, suddenly breaking silence. Whether his meditations were so intense as to be disturbed by the dog's winking, or whether his feelings were so wrought upon by his reflections that they required all the relief derivable from kicking an unoffending animal to allay them, is matter for argument and consideration. Whatever was the cause, the effect was a kick and a curse, bestowed
15 upon the dog simultaneously.

---

2 Write down the **discourse markers** that begin each section.

1 _____

2 _____

3 _____

Key term

Discourse marker: word or phrase used as an organizational tool to link ideas.

Think about how you can use similar discourse markers and structural features to organize your own description of a person or character. For example, you could start with the surroundings, then the character's appearance and then, finally, their relationship with a pet, or with another character.

Activity 10

Write a description of one of the following:

- an old lady in her front room with a cat on her lap
- a young child in the garden with a new puppy
- a parent and child out shopping.

Remember to use discourse markers and structural features to organize your description. Continue on blank paper if you need to.

The narrative task

What is narrative?

Unlike a stand-alone description, a narrative is built around a series of events. It is assessed against the same criteria but some are interpreted differently to take into account the features of an effective narrative.

For example:

- a well-described setting
- an engaging event which encourages the reader to continue reading
- convincing characters conveyed through description, thought, action or dialogue.

In Section B of Paper 1 you may be asked to write a whole short story or just a part, for example, the opening of a story or its ending. To produce a higher-grade response to the narrative task you will need to do the following.

Content

- ☐ Make sure the register you use in your story is convincing and compelling for your audience. Think about the kind of words and the manner of writing used. You can make anything happen in your narrative, as long as you make your reader believe it.
- ☐ Ensure that your writing is assuredly matched to purpose – for instance, think about the atmosphere you want to create in your story: is this tense or spooky?
- ☐ Craft your writing, using precise, sophisticated vocabulary and descriptive linguistic devices (such as reflecting the tone of your writing in the sound of the words that you've chosen or varying your sentence lengths to control the pace).

Organization

- ☐ Incorporate varied and effective structural features – for instance, include effective dialogue to convey character and move the narrative on.
- ☐ Incorporate a range of complex and convincing ideas to make your writing compelling – for instance, express a theme such as love or betrayal.
- ☐ Construct fluently linked paragraphs with seamlessly integrated discourse markers.

Technical accuracy

- ☐ Consistently demarcate your sentences securely and accurately.
- ☐ Use a wide range of punctuation with a high level of accuracy.
- ☐ Use a full range of appropriate sentence forms for effect.
- ☐ Use Standard English consistently and appropriately with secure control of complex grammatical structures.
- ☐ Achieve a high level of accuracy in spelling, including ambitious vocabulary.
- ☐ Use extensive and ambitious vocabulary.

Look back at your writing skills self-evaluation on pages 8–9 and tick the skills that you need to prioritize to achieve a higher grade.

Planning your narrative

The narrative task will provide a written prompt, scenario or visual image to act as a stimulus for your writing, so use this to help you to develop your ideas as you plan. Planning a story which will gain a higher grade involves taking some risks. As well as being technically accurate, the story must be convincing and well crafted.

Look at the following example task.

> **You have been asked to enter a creative writing competition judged by young people.**
>
> **Write a description suggested by this picture:**
>
>

Student A has come up with the following idea.

Student A

> A mother discovers that her small son or daughter has disappeared. Has the child been abducted?

To engage the reader, Student A has come up with a plot that disrupts the ordinary scene of the shopping centre by adding some drama.

Activity 1

1 Write the first two paragraphs of Student A's story from the mother's point of view, using either first-person or third-person narration. This section of writing should end with the discovery that the child is missing.

Think about the following:

- How will you control the change of mood between the relaxed shoppers and the sudden shock and fear?

- How will you establish the characters and their relationships?

Continue on blank paper if you need to.

Activity 2

1 Now write the next two or three paragraphs in which the mother (and any other characters) respond to the disappearance.

Think about the following:

- How you can present the mother's thoughts and feelings?

- What dialogue will you include? What will people say and how will she respond?

- How can you make your narrative convincing? Think about how people would react in this situation.

Characterization, description and action

To create a convincing and engaging narrative you need to interweave action with description in a way that tells the reader more about the characters and setting as the story progresses.

Read the following extract from Catherine O'Flynn's novel *What Was Lost*. Here, the main character Kate is in a communal playground.

Activity 3

Using three different colours, highlight the passage to identify:

- words and phrases that describe the playground and the estate

- words and phrases that describe the storm

- words and phrases which describe Kate's thoughts, feelings and actions.

> **Extract from *What Was Lost* by Catherine O'Flynn**
> --
>
> Kate ran over the brow of the artificial hill. The sky was purple behind her and a gale blasted the ugly, spindly trees, bending and flicking their branches. The litter had escaped from the shrubs and now whipped in cyclones in the doorways of the maisonettes.
> 5 A thunder- storm was coming and Kate could feel the air fizzing and sparking as she ran through it. The wind blew her faster as she leapt down the slope and ran and ran. She felt unbreakable as she ran past the shattered glass of the bus stop, over the landscaped undulations of the estate and through the deserted
> 10 quadrangle. Washing snapped crazily on the lines in the quad and Kate ran through it blindly, breathing in the floral detergent as sheets wrapped around her face. She laughed and ran, past the school, past the shabby, kit-built Methodist church, leaping as she ran, feeling out of control, hoping that the wind would carry her
> 15 off. As the first, fat blobs of rain splatted on the pavement she was running down her road. She wanted to get up to her window to watch the coming lightning sweep across the wires of the pylons.

Note how at least two colours are present in most sentences.

Activity 4

1 Think about how a different character, walking through an estate, might react to the same thunder storm described in the extract on page 69. This might be:

- a young parent with a toddler
- an old man or woman with a heavy bag of shopping
- a young man or woman on their way to an important job interview
- the organizer of a school fete, on their way to the event.

How might the character and their situation affect the description of the storm?

2 Write a section of a narrative describing your chosen character's experience of the thunder storm. Continue on blank paper if you need to.

3 Using two different colours, highlight your writing to identify action and description. Check that you have interweaved action with description in a way that tells the reader more about the character.

Opening your narrative

In the exam, the opening of your story is crucial. It must be creative and engaging as this sets the standard in the examiner's mind. The examiner will begin to form an opinion of your writing from the first word so you need to show your control and flair in the first few paragraphs.

Activity 5

Read the opening of *The Unlikely Pilgrimage of Harold Fry* by Rachel Joyce. As you read, think about the way that the writing is structured. You should look at:

- the opening sentence
- physical descriptions of setting and characters
- how characters' thoughts are presented
- how dialogue is used.

Annotate this passage to identify how the author has used these features to create an effective opening.

Extract from *The Unlikely Pilgrimage of Harold Fry* by Rachel Joyce

---

The letter that would change everything arrived on a Tuesday. It was an ordinary morning in mid-April that smelled of clean washing and grass cuttings. Harold Fry sat at the breakfast table, freshly shaved, in a clean shirt and tie, with a slice of toast that he wasn't eating. He gazed beyond the kitchen window at the clipped lawn, which was spiked in the middle by Maureen's telescopic washing line, and trapped on all three sides by the neighbours' stockade fencing.

"Harold!" called Maureen above the vacuum cleaner. "Post!"

He thought he might like to go out, but the only thing to do was mow the lawn and he had done that yesterday. The vacuum tumbled into silence, and his wife appeared, looking cross, with a letter. She sat opposite Harold.

Maureen was a slight woman with a cap of silver hair and a brisk walk. When they first met, nothing had pleased him more than to make her laugh. To watch her neat frame collapse into unruly happiness. "It's for you," she said. He didn't know what she meant until she slid an envelope across the table, and stopped it just short of Harold's elbow. They both looked at the letter as if they had never seen one before. It was pink. "The postmark says Berwick-upon-Tweed."

He didn't know anyone in Berwick. He didn't know many people anywhere. "Maybe it's a mistake."

"I think not. They don't get something like a postmark wrong." She took toast from the rack. She liked it cold and crisp.

Look again at the two short sentences at the end of the passage:

'She took toast from the rack. She liked it cold and crisp.'

This is a very neat writer's trick that you can use in your own writing. Although the words cold and crisp only seem to apply to the toast, a reader will understand immediately that they also apply to Maureen. Think about how your character's actions can reveal to the reader something about their personality.

Activity 6

Write the opening of a narrative where a character or characters in a normal everyday situation have to react to an unexpected communication (for example, a phone call, letter, email or text).

You should structure your opening in a similar way to the extract opposite, including dialogue and description to establish your characters and setting. Continue on blank paper if you need to.

Exam tip

When writing in the exam, don't create too many characters as this can complicate your narrative and make it difficult to control. Try to restrict yourself to one main character and two or three supporting characters.

72

Structuring your narrative

When developing your narrative, you need to use a range of structural features creatively and effectively in order to attain the higher grades. Some structural features you can use include:

- opening with dialogue rather than description or action

- switching narrative perspective (possibly presenting two contrasting perspectives of the same event)

- shifts in time, location or focus (for example, moving closer in to the action)

- varying the narrative pace of the section, that is, how quickly or slowly you take the reader through the action

- **flashback** (for example, the narrator or main character recalls a past event which is then described as if it is happening now before the narrative returns to the present).

Study the picture below. Imagine an old woman or man looking out of the window at this scene.

Key term

Flashback: an episode in a narrative that tells an earlier part of the story.

To make a flashback work effectively you need to think about how to make the transition from the present to the past and then possibly back again.

Activity 7

Read the first section of Student C's flashback story based on the picture on page 73.

Annotate Student C's response to identify the following structural features:

- a link between the present and the past
- contrast between age and youth
- a character's thoughts presented as if spoken aloud
- use of ellipsis to indicate time shift to the past.

Student C

Beryl drew back the net curtain and scrubbed the condensation from the window. The snow had fallen steadily over night and now it lay thick on the cobbles, muffling the early morning sounds. It was so quiet, as if the whole world was still asleep but it was still early, of course. She didn't sleep so well these days, with the pain in her hip.

She felt that something was wrong with the scene. What could it be? Of course! There were no children out to enjoy the snow. That's what was needed – the sound of children laughing and playing!

As she stood by the window, her hand still holding the curtain, she began to hear the laughter...

Activity 8

Write the next few paragraphs in which you establish Beryl as a child. You might have her out playing in the snow or watching through the window while other children play. Think about how you will convey the shift in time to the reader. Continue on blank paper.

Activity 9

Write the opening three paragraphs of a narrative in response to the following written prompt:

> Write a story about a family holiday.

You should use one or more of the structural features identified in the bullet-point list at the top of the opposite page. You could base your narrative on one of the following suggestions or use your own idea.

- Two parents set off on their first family holiday with very young children.

- An old man or woman watches a young family leaving on holiday.

- A teenager is coerced into going on a family holiday when really he or she wanted to stay at home alone.

- An adult finds an old photograph of one of their childhood holidays.

Technical accuracy

In Section B of Paper 1, you will be awarded up to 24 marks for AO5 (composition and organization) but don't forget that there are 16 marks available for AO6 (technical accuracy). To ensure that you gain as many marks for AO6 as possible, make sure that you:

- re-read your writing as you go and leave enough time for a final proofread at the end
- remember to check that you have used a wide range of punctuation accurately
- use a range of sophisticated vocabulary
- use a range of sentence structures for effect.

Activity 10

Look back at your response to Activity 9 on page 75.

1 Read through the response focusing only on the vocabulary that you used. Underline any words that you consider to be sophisticated. These don't have to be long or complex, but they should be precise and well chosen.

2 Now read through the response again, this time focusing on sentence types. Do you vary your sentence lengths? Do you open your sentences in different ways? Does the pace of your writing change?

3 Make any changes that you think would improve the mark this response would receive for AO6.

Exam tip

To improve the technical accuracy of your writing under exam conditions, give yourself five AO6 'lives' when you check any written response that you have written under timed conditions. When you have completed and proofread your response, hand it to your teacher or another student. Every spelling, punctuation or grammatical error they identify loses you a 'life'. This will help you to identify the type of mistakes you make and eliminate these from your writing.

45
inutes

Activity 11

Now that you have practised your descriptive and narrative writing skills, it's time to put them all together as you write a complete response to an example Paper 1 Section B writing task. Choose the form of writing that you find more difficult so that you can practise it.

You are going to write for the creative section of a general interest magazine aimed at people of your own age.

Either:

Write a description suggested by this picture:

Or:

Write the opening part of a story about a charity event.

Start your writing below and continue on blank paper.

Progress check

Now that you have practised the skills needed for a higher-grade response to a Paper 1 Section B writing task, carry out the progress check below and on the facing page. Use three highlighter pens of different colours to highlight passages of your answer to Activity 11 to show where you have satisfied each of the criteria for a higher grade.

Paper/AO	Skills	Basic skills descriptors	Check ✓	Target higher grade skills descriptors	Check ✓
Paper 1 AO5	Communicate clearly, effectively and imaginatively	I can communicate my ideas successfully most of the time.		I can communicate my ideas convincingly, affecting the reader's response.	
	Select and adapt tone, style and register	I have some control of the tone, style and register of my writing and they are usually appropriate.		I am confident in adopting and sustaining an appropriate tone, style and register for my writing to achieve subtle effects.	
		I can use a variety of vocabulary and some linguistic devices in my writing.		I can use an extensive and ambitious vocabulary, crafting a range of linguistic devices to achieve effects.	
	Organize ideas	I have a variety of relevant ideas in my writing and can make links between them.		I can develop and integrate complex and engaging ideas in my writing.	
	Use structural and grammatical features	I can use paragraphs to organize my writing and sometimes use discourse markers.		I can link paragraphs coherently and fluently using integrated discourse markers.	
		I can use some structural features in my writing.		I can use a variety of structural features creatively and effectively.	

 # My target skills

List any AO5 skills you need to improve the reach the higher grade skills descriptors.

1 _____

2 _____

3 _____

4 _____

5 _____

Use this self-evaluation to help you to plan your work, so that you spend most of your time targeting the skills that you most need to develop.

Paper/AO	Skills	Basic skills descriptors	Check ✔	Target higher grade skills descriptors	Check ✔
Paper 1 AO6	Demarcation and punctuation	I usually write in full sentences and can use full stops and capital letters accurately.		I consistently use a range of punctuation to demarcate my sentences accurately.	
		I can use some punctuation marks, for example, question marks and speech marks.		I can use a wide range of punctuation with a very high level of accuracy.	
	Sentence forms and Standard English	I can sometimes use different sentence forms in my writing, for example, rhetorical questions.		I can use a full range of sentence forms in my writing to achieve specific effects on the reader.	
		I usually write sentences which are grammatically correct and can use some Standard English.		I can write and control sentences with complex grammatical structures and consistently use Standard English.	
	Spelling and vocabulary	I can spell basic words and some more complex words accurately.		I can spell most words accurately, including more ambitious words.	
		I can use a variety of vocabulary, including some complex words.		I can use an extensive and ambitious range of vocabulary.	

My target skills

List any AO6 skills you need to improve the reach the higher grade skills descriptors.

1 --

2 --

3 --

4 --

5 --

Use this self-evaluation to help you to plan your work, so that you spend most of your time targeting the skills that you most need to develop.

Paper 2: Writers' viewpoints and perspectives

Overview of the exam paper

This exam lasts 1 hour 45 minutes and the exam paper is split into
two sections.

- Section A: Reading

  - In this section you will read *two non-fiction texts*, one from the 19th
    century and one from either the 20th or 21st centuries and show your
    understanding of how writers from different time periods and genres
    present a perspective or viewpoint to influence the reader.

  - You will have to answer four questions.

  - This section is worth 40 marks.

- Section B: Writing

  - In this section you will write your own text to a specified audience,
    purpose and form in which you give your perspective on the theme
    that has been introduced in Section A.

  - This section is worth 40 marks.

How your reading will be marked

Below is a table that reminds you of the Assessment Objectives (AOs) that
you will be tested on in the reading section of Paper 2.

Assessment Objective	The reading skills that you need to demonstrate
AO1	Identify and interpret explicit and implicit information and ideas. Select and synthesize evidence from different texts.
AO2	Explain, comment on and analyse how writers use language and structure to achieve effects and influence readers, using relevant subject terminology to support your views.
AO3	Compare writers' ideas and perspectives, as well as how these are conveyed, across two or more texts.

By working through the following chapter, you will practise these skills
and learn exactly how and where to demonstrate them in the Paper 2 exam
in order to achieve the higher grades.

How your writing will be marked

Your writing will be marked against two Assessment Objectives:

Assessment Objective	The writing skills that you need to demonstrate
AO5 (Content and organization)	Communicate clearly, effectively and imaginatively, selecting and adapting tone, style and register for different forms, purposes and audiences.
	Organize information and ideas, using structural and grammatical features to support coherence and cohesion of texts.
AO6 (Technical accuracy)	Use a range of vocabulary and sentence structures for clarity, purpose and effect, with accurate spelling and punctuation.

Overall, the writing question in Paper 2 is worth a maximum of 40 marks: 24 marks are available for content and organization (AO5); 16 marks are available for technical accuracy (AO6).

What is content and organization?

To gain good marks for content and organization you need to get your ideas across to the reader clearly and match your writing to whatever purpose, audience and form is required.

You will need to make conscious choices of language and textual features, so that your writing has the intended impact on readers. To assess this, the examiner will look at the way you use individual words and phrases, as well as the way you sequence, link and present your writing. The structure of your whole piece of writing, and of paragraphs and sections within it, will be taken into account.

What is technical accuracy?

Technical accuracy is using words, punctuation and grammar correctly. Your writing needs to show that you can use a range of vocabulary in correctly punctuated sentences, written in Standard English. Accuracy in spelling and punctuation will be taken into account, as well as your control over sentence structure. This doesn't just mean forming sentences correctly, but also means using a variety of sentence structures for different purposes and effects in a controlled way.

Question 1

Identifying explicit and implicit information and ideas

This question assesses your ability to identify specific information and ideas that are either straightforwardly stated in a set section of the source text or can be inferred or deduced from it.

You will be asked to identify **four** true statements from a list of eight. Some of the statements that you will encounter in this question will be inferred or deduced from the text, rather than explicitly stated. In order to establish whether they are true or not, you will need to read the text carefully and test each statement against your understanding of the evidence presented in the set section of the source text.

Generally, Question 1 doesn't present most higher-level students with a great deal of challenge. However you need to be aware of the following possible pitfalls:

- This is the first question, so you might be nervous.

- You may think of this question as easy and be tempted to rush it.

- Some of the information presented in the statements needs to be inferred or deduced from the text, so you might wrongly identify a true statement as false or vice versa.

As you are aiming for a higher grade, you should be able to gain full marks (4) for this question.

An important feature of this question is that some statements are likely to contain information that is not stated directly in the text.

Look at the following headline from the newspaper article on the opposite page:

> # An audience with Koko the 'talking' gorilla

Referring to the headline only, do you think the following statement is true or false?

A   Koko the gorilla can speak.   ⬭

The answer is that it is false. That is because although the words might lead you to think that Koko can speak, the use of quotation marks around the word 'talk' implies that the 'talking' doesn't involve uttering words. She communicates by other means.

An audience with Koko the 'talking' gorilla

My location is a closely guarded secret: a ranch somewhere in the Santa Cruz Mountains, several miles outside the small California town of Woodside. And for good reason, for its resident is something of a celebrity. She lives here with a male friend and both value their privacy, so much so
5 that I'm asked to keep absolutely silent as I walk the single-track dirt path that winds through a grove of towering redwoods up to a little Portakabin.

Inside, I'm asked to put on a thin medical mask to cover my nose and mouth and a pair of latex gloves. Then my guide, Lorraine, tells me to follow another dirt trail to a different outbuilding. This one has a small wooden
10 porch attached and it's here that I sit on a plastic chair and look up at an open door, separated from the outside world by a wire fence that stretches the length and width of the frame. And there she is: Koko. A 300lb lowland gorilla, sitting staring back at me and pointing to an impressive set of teeth.

I'd been told beforehand not to make eye contact initially as it can be
15 perceived as threatening, and so I glare at the ground. But I can't help stealing brief glances at this beautiful creature.

Koko, if you're not familiar, was taught American sign language when she was about a year old. Now 40, she apparently has a working vocabulary of more than 1,000 signs and understands around 2,000 words of spoken
20 English. Forty years on, the Gorilla Foundation's Koko project has become the longest continuous inter-species communications programme of its kind anywhere in the world.

I sign "hello", which looks like a sailor's salute, and she emits a long, throaty growl. "Don't worry, that means she likes you," comes the disembodied
25 voice of Dr Penny Patterson, the foundation's president and scientific director, from somewhere inside the enclosure. "It's the gorilla equivalent of a purr." Koko grins at me, then turns and signs to Dr Patterson. "She wants to see your mouth… wait, she particularly wants to see your tongue," Dr Patterson says, and I happily oblige, pulling my mask down, poking my
30 tongue out and returning the grin.

> **Key term**
>
> **Implicit:** information and ideas that are not directly stated in the text. Readers must infer or deduce them by using their knowledge and understanding of the text and their life experiences.

Activity 1

Re-read lines 1–16 and devise two true statements about this text. One should be explicit (stated in the text); the other should be implicit. Explain the evidence for your implicit statement.

Explicit statement: _____

Implicit statement: _____

Evidence to support this: _____

_____

The following statements are based on implicit information from lines 1–16 of the text.

Statement	Evidence
The gorillas are disturbed by noise.	The journalist is asked to keep absolutely silent as he walks towards the gorilla.
The scientists are concerned that germs might be passed either to or from the gorillas.	He is asked to put on a thin medical mask to cover his nose and mouth and a pair of latex gloves.
The gorillas' location is kept secret because otherwise members of the public might disturb them.	Koko is 'something of a celebrity' and so people might want to see her.

Activity 2

Look back at your answer to Activity 1 on page 83. Discuss any differences between the implicit statement you devised and the statements presented in the table above.

Read the letter on the opposite page and complete the activity below. The letter appeared in the 'Family' section of *The Guardian* newspaper as part of a series in which readers are encouraged to write an imaginary letter to someone important in their life.

5 minutes

Activity 3

Read the letter again, from lines 1 to 24.

Choose **four** statements below that are true.

- Shade the boxes of the ones that you think are true.

- Choose a maximum of four statements.

A	The writer hates death metal music.	⬭
B	The writer's son is able to drive.	⬭
C	The writer's son plays in a band.	⬭
D	The writer finds many of her son's habits irritating.	⬭
E	The writer and her son never argue.	⬭
F	The writer's son is sometimes absent-minded.	⬭
G	The writer's son likes playing loud music.	⬭
H	The writer's son goes to bed early.	⬭

A letter to my son, who is leaving home

You are 19; we've lived together long enough and there are many things that I will not miss when you go. I will not miss the peace of the house being shattered by music that sounds like a Viking
5 murdering a walrus with a chainsaw. I will not miss death metal being played through speakers on the landing so you can hear it while you are in the bath; I will not miss you explaining that it's not death metal but post-hardcore, when it's the volume not the sub-genre that's the issue. I will not miss your bass reverberating
10 through the house at midnight – or at 6am; I will not miss your band choosing to name themselves after a serial killer; I will not miss driving you to a derelict building at the end of a darkened alley for rehearsals; I will not miss your amp being hauled in and out of the boot of the car.

15 I will not miss the 10-mile round trip to pick you up from your girlfriend's house when you've split up and the last bus has just left; I will not miss the 10-mile round trip back to your girlfriend's house because you and she made up via text during the previous journey.

20 I will not miss you staring blankly ahead when I am speaking to you when you have your headphones in; I will not miss you uncorking one of your headphones and roaring "What?" when I repeat myself; I will not miss having to raise my voice and turning a straightforward conversation into a shouted confrontation [...]

25 I will not miss you picking up and wandering off with household essentials: scissors, tweezers, corkscrews, the remote control. I will not miss you indignantly claiming you never touched them, and being mystified and outraged when they turn up in your room.

I will not miss you dismissing the range of conventional breakfast
30 foods that are crammed into the fridge, then telling me you're in the mood for sushi. I will not miss you sighing that you're sick of chicken and that I never put enough chilli in anything. I will not miss you eating all the ice cream; I will not miss you reducing the kitchen to rubble by the simple act of making a peanut butter
35 sandwich [...]

I will not miss the slammed doors, the wet towels, the abrupt and unrequested change of channels when I'm watching the news; I will not miss the jumble of enormous shoes by the back door; I will not miss the trail of mugs that chart your movements around
40 the house. I will not miss you bickering with your sister; I will not miss you wearing your hat at the table. I will not miss the snorts of derision when I offer my opinion or advice.

I will not miss any of the above.

I will miss you.

45 Love, Mum x

Check your answer to Activity 3 on page 84 against the list of correct true statements given below.

C   The writer's son plays in a band.

D   The writer finds many of her son's habits irritating.

F   The writer's son is sometimes absent-minded.

G   The writer's son likes playing loud music.

Progress check

Reflect on your answer to Activity 3 and use the following checklist to assess your progress.

	Yes	No
Did you read the statements very carefully to make sure that you understood them before you chose?		
Did you re-read the text to make sure that you had not misinterpreted it?		
Did you check that you had only chosen four statements?		
Would you have been awarded full marks for this question?		

Question 2

This question assesses your ability to select information and ideas from two texts and **synthesize** them into a coherent answer. To produce a higher-grade response you will need to:

- make *perceptive* inferences from both texts
- make *judicious* references/use of textual detail *relevant* to the focus of the question
- offer statements that show *perceptive* similarities or differences between the texts.

Activity 1

Look back at the qualities of a higher-grade response to Question 2 listed above, focusing in particular on the words in italics which are the skills that differentiate a higher-level response from a weaker answer.

Using a dictionary, write a clear definition for each of the italicised terms. Remember to think about what each word or phrase means in the context of answering Question 2.

Perceptive _____

_____

Judicious _____

_____

Relevant _____

_____

Exam tip

Remember that for this question you will need to re-read the whole of both texts, focusing on a specific aspect. You might be asked to write a summary of the similarities or differences between them. One key skill that is only assessed in Question 2 is the ability to synthesize evidence between these texts.

You will need to refer to Source A on the opposite page and Source B on page 90 to answer the following question.

> Use details from **both** sources to write a summary of the differences between the lives of the son and Sarah the 'slavey'.

When you start planning your answer to this question, you need to decide on two or three aspects of the texts that allow you to summarize the differences effectively. These decisions are crucial to the success of your answer, so it's worth thinking carefully about which aspects of both texts you will focus on.

Exam tip

The aspects you choose can be a useful way of organizing your answer. You could write a paragraph for each aspect, synthesizing evidence from both texts to show a detailed understanding of the differences between them.

Activity 2

Read Source A and Source B and decide on which aspects of the son's and Sarah's lives you could focus on in order to summarize the differences between them. Note down three aspects you could focus your answer on below.

1 _____

2 _____

3 _____

Activity 3

Re-read Source A and use the following table to collect information about the son's life. Splitting the information into these aspects allows you to examine the son's life in detail.

Social life	Home life and relationships	Economic situation
He plays in a band.		

Source A

A letter to my son, who is leaving home

You are 19; we've lived together long enough and there are many things that I will not miss when you go. I will not miss the peace of the house being shattered by music that sounds like a Viking

5 murdering a walrus with a chainsaw. I will not miss death metal being played through speakers on the landing so you can hear it while you are in the bath; I will not miss you explaining that it's not death metal but post-hardcore, when it's the volume not the sub-genre that's the issue. I will not miss your bass reverberating

10 through the house at midnight – or at 6am; I will not miss your band choosing to name themselves after a serial killer; I will not miss driving you to a derelict building at the end of a darkened alley for rehearsals; I will not miss your amp being hauled in and out of the boot of the car.

15 I will not miss the 10-mile round trip to pick you up from your girlfriend's house when you've split up and the last bus has just left; I will not miss the 10-mile round trip back to your girlfriend's house because you and she made up via text during the previous journey.

20 I will not miss you staring blankly ahead when I am speaking to you when you have your headphones in; I will not miss you uncorking one of your headphones and roaring "What?" when I repeat myself; I will not miss having to raise my voice and turning a straightforward conversation into a shouted confrontation.

25 I will not miss you picking up and wandering off with household essentials: scissors, tweezers, corkscrews, the remote control. I will not miss you indignantly claiming you never touched them, and being mystified and outraged when they turn up in your room.

I will not miss you dismissing the range of conventional breakfast

30 foods that are crammed into the fridge, then telling me you're in the mood for sushi. I will not miss you sighing that you're sick of chicken and that I never put enough chilli in anything. I will not miss you eating all the ice cream; I will not miss you reducing the kitchen to rubble by the simple act of making a peanut butter

35 sandwich.

I will not miss the slammed doors, the wet towels, the abrupt and unrequested change of channels when I'm watching the news; I will not miss the jumble of enormous shoes by the back door; I will not miss the trail of mugs that chart your movements around

40 the house. I will not miss you bickering with your sister; I will not miss you wearing your hat at the table. I will not miss the snorts of derision when I offer my opinion or advice.

I will not miss any of the above.

I will miss you.

45 Love, Mum x

Source B

Sarah the Slavey

LONDON girls of the lowest class have a strong prejudice against domestic service. Mothers are, as a rule, glad to see their girls in "a tidy little place." They realise that good food is necessary for a girl while she is growing, and that street life is very **pernicious**.
5 But the girls often prefer to live at home, even if it means drudgery that keeps them occupied from morning till night, blows, and drunken parents. The routine of service **tries** them very much, and they miss the companionship of school friends, brothers and
10 sisters. They complain of "lonesomeness." [...]

The girl who was placed six months ago in the house of a major in Kensington, is a fair type of the ordinary **slavey**. Her father rents two cellars near Lisson Grove. He is out of work, and only able to scrape along with the assistance of his wife, who is a
15 **charwoman**. He has six children. The eldest girl works in a factory, and earns four shillings and sixpence per week. Sarah is nearly fifteen, but looks like a child of twelve, because she is small and thin, the result of constant starving. Her father is a very respectable man, although out of work, having been employed in a
20 shop for many years. He now does odd jobs and runs errands. He was very anxious to find Sarah "a tidy little place," and delighted that she should go to service. The day on which this was arranged the mother lay in bed with the two youngest children because her clothes were in the pawnshop. The father had applied for relief to
25 the parish. So money was given to buy Sarah some clothes; and the girl was transported from her wretched home to the house in Kensington.

At first she was delighted with everything. She worked hard, and tried "to give satisfaction." The father called, and seemed pleased
30 to see the child so happy. But from the first she complained of "lonesomeness." She would not answer the back-door bell after dark, or sleep by herself. She cried when the cook left her alone in the kitchen. Then she began to mope, and said that she wanted her brothers and sisters, that she was sure her mother was ill, and
35 that she felt ill herself. She begged for pocket-money, saying that her mother had given her a few pence on a Saturday night. She asked to go out by herself, instead of with another servant. Last of all she ran away, having received a shilling from some-one in the house, and permission from the cook to fetch a stamp. She
40 preferred her wretched home, in which she had not enough to eat, to the house in Kensington, and now works ten hours a day in a factory, and gets two shillings and sixpence a week. She received the kindest treatment, and her life in the house of the Major was very different to that of most slaveys. But she was home-sick.

Glossary

pernicious – having a harmful effect

tries – used here to mean 'tests'

slavey – young maidservant

charwoman – cleaner

Activity 4

1 Look again at Source B and complete the following table to compile information about Sarah's life.

Social life	Home life and relationships	Economic situation

2 Look back at your completed tables in Activities 3 and 4 and think about the differences between the lives of the son in Source A and Sarah the 'slavey' in Source B.

Identifying perceptive differences

In order to achieve the highest marks on this question, you need to show a perceptive understanding of differences between the ideas and information you select from each text.

In Source A and Source B one of the biggest differences between the two teenagers' lives is their economic situation. Sarah's home life was poverty-stricken but to achieve high marks you need to do more than simply state this.

Activity 5

1 Re-read Source B and find three details that show that Sarah's home life was poverty-stricken. The first detail has been provided for you.

1 Her father is out of work.

2

3

2 Now re-read Source A and find three details to show that the son's economic situation is quite different to Sarah's.

1

2

3

3 Look back at your completed tables in Activities 3 and 4. Add any further evidence that will help you to demonstrate a perceptive understanding of the differences between the son's and Sarah's lives.

Make perceptive inferences

In order to achieve the highest marks for Question 2, you need to make perceptive inferences from both texts in your response to the question set. This means going beyond the information that is stated explicitly to make insightful interpretations of the implicit evidence you identify. You can build the inferences you make about different pieces of evidence into a perceptive interpretation of a specific difference between the two texts.

Read the following statements about the son from Source A and Sarah from Source B. Both of these statements make a perceptive inference of evidence from the texts.

1 The son displays behaviour that is often regarded as typical of modern teenagers.	2 Sarah felt that the relationship with her family was more important to her than her own comfort.

Activity 6

Devise four more perceptive statements about both texts. Two statements should be about the son's life and the other two about Sarah's life. Remember your statement should be based on inferences you have made from evidence in the texts.

1 -

2 -

3 -

4 -

Synthesizing evidence to make statements

Look again at the example Question 2 you are answering:

> Use details from **both** sources to write a summary of the differences between the lives of the son and Sarah the 'slavey'.

Think about the focus of this question: a summary of the differences between the lives of the son and Sarah the 'slavey'. In the exam, the Question 2 you face on Paper 2 may ask you to focus on similarities or differences. Whichever you are asked for, you need to synthesize relevant evidence from both texts into statements that show perceptive similarities or differences between the texts.

Here is an extract from a student's answer to the example Question 2 on page 92. This part of the answer focuses on the differences between the home lives of the son and Sarah the 'slavey'. The answer has been annotated to show how the information has been synthesized to form a coherent summary.

Student A

Topic sentence to open the paragraph and signal its contents

Linking phrase to introduce the other source

A complex sentence combining points about both sources to sum up.

The two teenagers' home lives and family relationships are also quite different. We sense that the son in Source A is ready to leave home and become independent; many of the selfish acts listed by his mother (e.g. playing loud music and making a mess) are classic symptoms of a young person wanting to live an independent life and feeling confined by family life. Sarah, on the other hand, is not ready to leave home and soon becomes homesick. We are told that 'she began to mope' and even 'felt ill'. Despite the fact that her home life was impoverished, she still preferred the company of her family; whereas the son seems to be quite resentful of family life, 'bickering' with his sister and having 'shouted' confrontations with his mother, giving 'snorts of derision' when she tries to give advice.

Useful phrase to indicate interpretation

Integrated quotes

Activity 7

Complete the tables below and over the page to combine your notes on the other two aspects of the son's and Sarah's lives.

Think about how you can synthesize the evidence you select to develop perceptive statements showing differences between their lives.

Social life	
Source A	**Source B**

Activity 7 *continued*

Economic situation	
Source A	Source B

Make judicious references/use of textual detail from both texts

When answering Question 2, it can be very easy to focus on one of the source texts over the other. You need to ensure you select **judicious references** or use textual details from *both* texts to support your answer.

To achieve the highest marks for this question you need to use quotations and references relevant to the focus of the question. To ensure you make judicious references/use of textual detail, you should practise:

- selecting only the words and phrases from each text which most effectively support each point

- integrating your quotations or references so that they fit in with the grammatical structure of your sentence.

Key term

Judicious references: carefully chosen quotation or example

Exam tip

The following discourse markers can be used to help you to synthesize information:

On the other hand...	In the same way...
Although...	We are told that...
Whereas...	We can assume that...
However...	The writer explains that...
Unlike...	We learn that...
Similarly...	We sense that...

Activity 8

Look back at your completed tables for Activity 7. Using the notes you made, write your own answer to the exam question below.

> Use details from **both** sources to write a summary of the differences between the lives of the son and Sarah the 'slavey'.

Before you begin to write your answer, look back at the extract from Student A's answer on page 93. Think about how you can follow this example to:

- make perceptive inferences from both texts
- offer a perceptive interpretation of the information
- select judicious quotes from each text that can be integrated into your answer.

Try to use discourse markers to guide the examiner through your answer as you write this on the opposite page.

Begin your answer here and continue on blank paper if you need to.

5
minutes

Activity 9

You need to refer to Source A on pages 97–98 and Source B on pages 98–99 for this question:

Use details from **both** sources. Write a summary of the differences between the experiences of a 20th century soldier and a 19th century soldier as described in the two extracts.

Begin your answer here and continue on blank paper if you need to.

Source A

Close calls

I had been shot at. More accurately, shots had been fired in my direction from afar, without effect on me or the men I was with. Mortars had fallen in my neighbourhood – none of them very close.

5 I'd travelled in convoys where other men got blown up by mines and been in a helicopter that got hit, but not punctured, by machine gun fire (Sergeant Benet and I felt the bullets pounding against the metal under our feet and gaped at each other in naked horror as our door gunner giggled and blasted away with his own machine gun). None of

10 these were close calls. A close call is personal, mysterious, sometimes fantastic. A bullet enters a man's helmet center-front and exits center-rear without putting a scratch on him. A platoon gets ambushed and overrun, after which the enemy puts a round in every man's head save one. A medic falls unnoticed from a pitching helicopter a thousand

15 yards up and lands feetfirst in a rice paddy, plunging to his neck in the mud, where an American patrol rescues him, entirely by accident, the next morning. Things like this happened every day, and the best stories got written up in Stars and Stripes with a picture of the lucky guy. My own close calls were pretty thin gruel by comparison but good

20 enough for me.

After mass Sergeant Benet and I drove to the village market to buy some fresh bread and vegetables. While he did the shopping I leaned back in the passenger seat and closed my eyes. My mood was still churchy, sentimental, liquid. I hadn't slept much the night before, and

25 now, surrounded by friendly indecipherable voices and warmed by the sun, I began to nod off. Then I became aware that the voices had stopped. The silence disturbed me. I sat up and looked around. The crowd had drawn back in a wide circle. They were staring at me. A woman yammered something I couldn't follow and pointed under the

30 jeep. I bent down for a look. There, lying directly below my seat, was a hand grenade. The pin had been pulled. I straightened up and sat there for a while, barely breathing. Then I got out of the jeep and walked over to where everyone else was standing. We were still within the grenade's killing range, especially if it set off the gas tank, but I didn't

35 think of that any more than the others had. I didn't have a thought in my head. We just stood there like a bunch of fools.

Sergeant Benet appeared at the edge of the crowd.

"What's going on?" he said.

"There's a grenade under the jeep."

40 He turned and looked. "Oh, man," he said. He dropped the groceries and started pushing people back, his arms outstretched like a riot cop's. "Di di mau!" he kept saying. "Beat it! Beat it!" Finally they gave ground, except for a bunch of kids who surrounded him and refused to be driven off. They were laughing. I looked on. None of it seemed to

45 have anything to do with me.

Once the area was cleared Sergeant Benet told a couple of skittish villagers to stand watch until we could send someone to take care of the grenade; then we started walking back to the battalion. Along the way I found my legs acting funny. My knees wouldn't lock; I had to lean against a wall. Sergeant Benet put his hand on my arm to steady me.

50

Source B

A report in *The Times* newspaper, written by William Howard Russell in 1854 from the front of the Crimean War, where British forces were fighting the Russian army. This event became famous as The Charge of the Light Brigade.

At 11:00 our Light Cavalry Brigade rushed to the front... The Russians opened on them with guns from the **redoubts** on the right, with volleys of musketry and rifles.

They swept proudly past, glittering in the morning sun in all the pride
5 and splendour of war. We could hardly believe the evidence of our senses. Surely that handful of men were not going to charge an army in position? Alas! It was but too true – their desperate valour knew no bounds. They advanced in two lines, quickening the pace as they closed towards the enemy. A more fearful spectacle was
10 never witnessed than by those who, without the power to aid, beheld their heroic countrymen rushing to the arms of sudden death. At the distance of 1200 yards the whole line of the enemy belched forth, from thirty iron mouths, a flood of smoke and flame through which hissed the deadly balls. Their flight was marked by instant gaps in
15 our ranks, the dead men and horses, by steeds flying wounded or riderless across the plain. The first line was broken – it was joined by the second, they never halted or checked their speed an instant. With diminished ranks, thinned by those thirty guns, which the Russians had laid with the most deadly accuracy, with a halo of flashing steel
20 above their heads, and with a cheer which was many a noble fellow's death cry, they flew into the smoke of the batteries; but 'ere they were lost from view, the plain was strewed with their bodies and with the carcasses of horses. They were exposed to an oblique fire from the batteries on the hills on both sides, as well as to a direct fire
25 of musketry.

Through the clouds of smoke we could see their sabres flashing as they rode up to the guns and dashed between them, cutting down the gunners as they stood. The blaze of their steel, like an officer standing near me said, "was like the turn of a shoal of mackerel." We saw them
30 riding through the guns, as I have said; to our delight, we saw them returning, after breaking through a column of Russian infantry and scattering them like chaff, when the flank fire of the battery on the hill swept them down, scattered and broken as they were. Wounded

men and dismounted troopers flying towards us told the sad tale –
35 demigods could not have done what they had failed to do. At the
very moment when they were about to retreat, a regiment of lancers
was hurled upon their flank. Colonel Shewell, of the 8th Hussars,
saw the danger and rode his men straight at them, cutting his way
through with fearful loss. The other regiments turned and engaged in
40 a desperate encounter. With courage too great almost for credence,
they were breaking their way through the columns which enveloped
them, where there took place an act of atrocity without parallel in
modern warfare of civilized nations. The Russian gunners, when the
storm of cavalry passed, returned to their guns. They saw their own
45 cavalry mingled with the troopers who had just ridden over them, and
to the eternal disgrace of the Russian name, the miscreants poured a
murderous volley of **grape and canister** on the mass of struggling
men and horses, mingling friend and foe in one common ruin. It was
as much as our Heavy Cavalry Brigade could do to cover the retreat of
50 the miserable remnants of that band of heroes as they returned to the
place they had so lately quitted in all the pride of life.

At 11:35 not a British soldier, except the dead and dying, was left in
front of those bloody **Muscovite** guns...

> **Glossary**
>
> **grape and canister** – different kinds of cannonball
>
> **Muscovite** – from Moscow in Russia

 # Progress check

Look back at your answer to Activity 9 and use the following checklist
to assess your progress. You could annotate your answer to pick out the
evidence that shows each skill.

		Yes	No
Identifying and Interpreting explicit and implicit information and ideas.	I can make **perceptive** inferences from both texts.		
Selecting and synthesizing evidence from different texts.	I can offer statements that show **perceptive** differences between texts.		
Supporting your ideas with appropriate textual references.	I can make **judicious** references/use of textual detail relevant to the focus of the question.		

Question 3

Understanding how a writer uses language

This question assesses your ability to analyse the effects of a writer's choices of language. To produce a higher-grade response you will need to:

- show *detailed and perceptive* understanding when you analyse the effects of the writer's choices of language

- make *sophisticated* and accurate use of subject terminology, linking references to language features to the results they produce

- select and use a *judicious range* of textual detail (i.e. quotations and examples) to support your analysis.

In the exam this question could relate to either Source A or Source B. When you answer this question, remember to read the source text closely, looking carefully for the following:

- words and phrases chosen for effect

- language features, for example, metaphor, simile, and so on

- sentence forms and patterns.

In your response, you will need to comment on and analyse the effects that these words and phrases, language features and sentence forms and patterns create in relation to the focus of the question.

> **Exam tip**
>
> This question could focus on a relatively short extract from one of the source texts. When you re-read the source text, slow your reading down and read forensically. Every phrase, word, piece of punctuation and sentence structure is likely to be important.

Analysis

As in Question 3 of Paper 1, the ability to analyse is the key to achieving high marks in Question 3 on Paper 2. You must show an understanding of the effects that the writer's choices of language have on the reader. So every time that you identify a relevant word, phrase, language feature or sentence form, ask yourself the following questions:

- Why has the writer chosen this?

- What effect does this language have on the reader?

Look at the following example Question 3.

> You now need to refer **only** to **Source B**, Russell's description of the charge (from lines 4 to 25).
>
> How does Russell use language to influence his readers into thinking that the charge was heroic?

This question is about Source B on pages 98-99, *The Times* newspaper report about 'The Charge of the Light Brigade'. The question asks how the writer uses language to influence readers into thinking the charge was heroic, focusing on lines 4–25 of the text.

Before you begin to analyse the extract, you need to consider what it is that the writer is trying to achieve in the report as a whole. William Howard Russell was a journalist at a time when there was no television or colour photography – even black and white photography was in its infancy. His job, then, was to describe the events as vividly as possible so that his readers could imagine them. However as a journalist on a British newspaper, William Howard Russell was not an impartial reporter on the war. The way he reports on 'The Charge of the Light Brigade' aims to manipulate his readers into a particular attitude to this event. In this case he wanted to make the Light Brigade out to be heroes, so chose his descriptive language to create that effect.

A student has annotated the first sentence of the extract, selecting words and phrases and analysing their effects.

> Powerful word. Like the sea or a river – they are like a natural force. The sound of the word 'swept' and 'past' contains repeated 's' and 't' mimicking the sound of the horses.

> Proudly – the word is picked up again later (pride). We can see them sitting upright in the saddle. This makes the reader feel proud of them because they represent their nation.

> Metal on their helmets, uniforms and swords has been polished, so they glitter like silver or gold. More like gods than men. They are not only brave but also beautiful.

> They swept proudly past, glittering in the morning sun in all the pride and splendour of war.

> The men are made to symbolise the beauty and nobility of war. 'Pride' is repeated for emphasis. This prepares us for his description of the charge. He wants us to see it as proud and splendid.

> A symbol of birth and hope. This makes their deaths even sadder.

Activity 1

Annotate the following sentences to analyse how Russell uses language to influence his readers into thinking that the charge was heroic.

Remember that you should analyse the use of punctuation and sentence forms as well as the words, phrases and language features.

> We could hardly believe the evidence of our senses. Surely that handful of men were not going to charge an army in position? Alas! It was but too true – their desperate valour knew no bounds.

Detailed and perceptive understanding

Once you have annotated the text, you should have a detailed understanding of the way the language has been used. But to achieve a high level, you need to show a perceptive response to the language too. One way to show this is to identify a single technique that underpins the choices that the writer has made. In Russell's report, that technique is **contrast**: the contrast between the noble, beautiful, brave soldiers and the horror of their deaths.

Key term

Contrast: where two opposite subjects are highlighted to emphasize their differences

Exam tip

A common mistake that students can make is to focus too much on effective words and phrases and ignore other relevant features. When you plan your answer to this question, make sure you analyse sentence forms, language features and punctuation as well.

Read Student B's answer focusing on the same section of text (lines 3–6).
It has been annotated to show how it could be seen to satisfy the
requirements for a Level 4 response.

Student B

At first, Russell describes the cavalry like heroes by creating a very strong visual image in the reader's mind, like a glowing painting. The soldiers 'swept' past as if they were a force of nature like a wave and the use of 'glittering' reinforces this idea, making them seem both beautiful and powerful. This is summed up in the word 'splendour' which encapsulates their power and beauty – they are like gods. He repeats the idea of pride in the sentence to emphasise it – encouraging the reader to see the soldiers as symbols of the 'pride and splendour of war'. The 'morning sun' gives the image a sense of hope which we know is doomed and this sense of doom is picked up by the rhetorical question, 'Surely that handful of men were not going to charge an army in position?', where the word 'handful' makes them suddenly seem weak and vulnerable – a total contrast to the previous image of power. Russell uses the question as an appeal to the reader to share his amazement and dread. He builds on this by using an emotional exclamation 'Alas' which expresses his fear and sadness as he responds to the sight. When he puts the intensifier 'too' in front of 'true', we sense his despair. The sight seemed unbelievable but these few brave men were actually going to charge the enemy – facing certain death. When he describes their valour as 'desperate' – a sad, depressing word – this is in stark contrast to the way the way their bravery was described at the start, all proud and glittering.

Detailed analysis of effects

A perceptive understanding

A judicious range of textual detail

A judicious range of textual detail

A judicious range of textual detail

A judicious range of textual detail

Perceptive understanding of language use

Exam tip

When answering Question 3 in the exam, think about the words and phrases you use to introduce each piece of analysis in order to form a coherent answer. You could use some of the following examples from Student B's response:

- At first...
- by creating…. in the reader's mind,
- making them seem…
- encouraging the reader to see…
- a total contrast to…
- He builds on this...
- which expresses…
- we sense…
- When he describes…

Sophisticated use of subject terminology

In order to achieve the highest marks on Question 3, you need to make sophisticated and accurate use of subject terminology in your response. Think about the focus of the question and link the references you make to different language features to the effects these create.

Here are three examples of subject terminology you could use to refer to specific language features used in Source B on pages 98–99:

- Personification – the use of human features, behaviours or characteristics to describe something that is inanimate

- Fronted adverbial – a phrase or clause that modifies a verb, which appears at the beginning of a sentence

- Juxtaposition – where two or more ideas are placed side by side in a text for the purpose of developing comparisons and contrasts.

Activity 2

Find examples of the three language features listed above in Source B on pages 98–99 and explain the effect each one creates. Try to focus your explanation on how this language feature influences readers into thinking the charge was heroic.

Personification _

_ _

_ _

_ _

_ _

Fronted adverbial _

_ _

_ _

_ _

_ _

Juxtaposition _

_ _

_ _

_ _

_ _

Activity 3

Look again at example Question 3.

> You now need to refer **only** to **Source B**, Russell's description of the charge (from lines 4 to 25).
>
> How does Russell use language to influence his readers into thinking that the charge was heroic?

Read the rest of the set section from Source B below (lines 8–25). As you read, annotate the text to identify relevant words and phrases, sentence forms and language features that will help you to answer the question. Remember to use subject terminology to identify these and to analyse them perceptively to explore the effects they have on the reader.

> They advanced in two lines, quickening the pace as they closed towards the enemy. A more fearful spectacle was never witnessed than by those who, without the power to aid, beheld their heroic countrymen rushing to the arms of sudden death. At the distance of 1200 yards the whole line of the enemy belched forth, from thirty iron mouths, a flood of smoke and flame through which hissed the deadly balls. Their flight was marked by instant gaps in our ranks, the dead men and horses, by steeds flying wounded or riderless across the plain. The first line was broken – it was joined by the second, they never halted or checked their speed an instant. With diminished ranks, thinned by those thirty guns, which the Russians had laid with the most deadly accuracy, with a halo of flashing steel above their heads, and with a cheer which was many a noble fellow's death cry, they flew into the smoke of the batteries; but 'ere they were lost from view, the plain was strewed with their bodies and with the carcasses of horses. They were exposed to an oblique fire from the batteries on the hills on both sides, as well as to a direct fire of musketry.

Activity 4

Write your answer to Question 3, focusing on the extract on the previous page. Remember to produce a higher-grade response you will need to:

- show *detailed and perceptive* understanding when you analyse the effects of the writer's choices of language

- make *sophisticated and accurate use of* subject terminology, linking references to language features to the results they produce

- select and use a *judicious range* of textual detail to support your analysis.

Begin your answer here and continue on blank paper if you need to.

In 1846, Charles Dickens visited a 'Ragged School' – a free school for children whose families were too poor to pay for education. Read the following extract from his letter to *The Daily News* newspaper describing his visit and then complete the activity on the next page.

Source A

It consisted at that time of either two or three – I forget which – miserable rooms, upstairs in a miserable house. In the best of these, the pupils in the female school were being taught to read and write; and though there were among the number, many wretched creatures
5   steeped in degradation to the lips, they were tolerably quiet, and listened with apparent earnestness and patience to their instructors. The appearance of this room was sad and melancholy, of course – how could it be otherwise! – but, on the whole, encouraging.

The close, low chamber at the back, in which the boys were crowded,
10   was so foul and stifling as to be, at first, almost insupportable. But its moral aspect was so far worse than its physical, that this was soon forgotten. Huddled together on a bench about the room, and shown out by some flaring candles stuck against the walls, were a crowd of boys, varying from mere infants to young men; sellers of fruit, herbs,
15   **lucifer-matches**, flints; sleepers under the dry arches of bridges; young thieves and beggars – with nothing natural to youth about them: with nothing frank, ingenuous, or pleasant in their faces; low-browed, vicious, cunning, wicked; abandoned of all help but this; speeding downward to destruction; and UNUTTERABLY IGNORANT [...]

20   This was the Class I saw at the Ragged School. They could not be trusted with books; they could only be instructed orally; they were difficult of reduction to anything like attention, obedience, or decent behaviour; their benighted ignorance in reference to the Deity, or to any social duty (how could they guess at any social duty, being so
25   discarded by all social teachers but the gaoler and the hangman!) was terrible to see. Yet, even here, and among these, something had been done already. The Ragged School was of recent date and very poor; but he had inculcated some association with the name of the Almighty, which was not an oath, and had taught them to look
30   forward in a hymn (they sang it) to another life, which would correct the miseries and woes of this.

Glossary

lucifer-matches
– lucifer-matches were the first cheap safety matches

Activity 5

You now need to refer **only** to **Source A**, Dickens' letter to a national newspaper (from the beginning to line 19).

How does Dickens use language to show his readers what a Ragged School was like?

Progress check

Look back at your answer to Activity 5 and use the following checklist to assess your progress. You could annotate your answer to pick out the evidence that shows each skill.

		Yes	No
Identifying and Interpreting explicit and implicit information and ideas.	I can show **detailed** understanding effects of the writer's choices of language.		
	I can show a **perceptive** understanding of the writer's choices of language.		
	I can **analyse** the effects of the writer's choices of language.		
Using relevant subject terminology to support your views	I can make **sophisticated** and **accurate** use of subject terminology.		
Supporting your ideas with appropriate textual references	I can support my ideas with a **judicious range** of textual detail.		

Question 4

Comparing writers' ideas and perspectives

Question 4 assesses your ability to compare the whole of both texts, focusing on the writers' ideas and perspectives and how they are conveyed. To produce a higher-grade response you will need to:

- compare ideas and perspectives in *a perceptive* way

- *analyse* how writers' methods are used

- select a range of *judicious* supporting detail from both texts.

- show a *detailed understanding* of the similarities and differences between the ideas and perspectives in both sources

You will now explore each of these key skills in turn to help you to build and develop the skills you need to produce a higher-grade response to Question 4.

This question is worth 16 marks (a high proportion of the marks on this paper) and it assesses all the skills that you have already employed separately to answer the other questions. This time, however, you have to bring them all together to compare two texts from different centuries.

Activity 1

Question 4 might ask you to compare how writers' convey their:

- ideas

- perspectives

- views or viewpoints

- experiences.

Using a dictionary, write a clear definition for each of the following phrases. Remember to think about what this phrase means in the context of answering Question 4.

Writer's ideas

Writer's perspective

Writer's viewpoint

Writer's experience

Identifying writers' attitudes and perspectives

When answering Question 4 in the exam, you need to make sure that you can identify and understand the perspective of the writer of each source text. To do this, you will need to read carefully to consider the context in which they are writing and how they convey their attitudes to the subject they are writing about.

Read the following extract from *Wild Life Under The Equator* by Paul Du Chaillu. Paul Du Chaillu was a zoologist who in 1862 travelled to West Africa, accompanied by local tribesmen, in search of gorillas. His aim was to kill a specimen and bring it back to Europe. As you read, think about what Du Chaillu's perspective on encountering the gorilla is and how he conveys his attitude towards the animal.

Source A

Hunting the gorilla

Suddenly Miengai uttered a little cluck with his tongue, which is the native's way of showing that something is stirring, and that a sharp look-out is necessary; in a word, to keep ourselves on our guard, or that danger was surrounding us. Presently I noticed,
5 ahead of us seemingly, a noise as of someone breaking down branches or twigs of trees.

We stopped and came close together. I knew at once, by the eager and satisfied looks of the men that it was a gorilla. They looked once more carefully at their guns, to see if by any chance the powder had fallen out of the pans; I also examined mine, to make sure that all were right, and then we marched on cautiously.

10 The singular noise of the breaking of the branches continued. We walked with the greatest care, making no noise at all. The countenances of the men showed that they thought themselves engaged in a very serious undertaking; but we pushed on, until I thought I could see through the woods the moving of the branches and small trees which the great beast was tearing down, probably to get from them the berries and
15 fruits he lives on [...]

Suddenly, as we were still creeping along, in a silence which made a heavy breath seem loud and distinct, the woods were at once filled with the tremendous barking roar of the gorilla.

Then the underbrush swayed rapidly ahead, and presently there stood before us an
20 immense male gorilla. He had come through the jungle on all-fours; but when he saw our party he stood up and looked us boldly in the face. He stood about a dozen yards from us, and it was a sight I shall never forget. Nearly six feet high, with immense body, huge chest, and great muscular arms, with fiercely–glaring large, deep, grey eyes, and a hellish expression of face, which seemed to me like some nightmare vision: thus stood
25 before me the king of the African forest. How black his face was!

He was not afraid of us. He stood there, and beat his breast with his huge fists till it resounded like an immense bass-drum, which is their mode of offering defiance; meantime giving vent to roar after roar. This roar was the most singular and awful noise I had ever heard in these African forests. It began with a sharp bark, like that of an angry
30 dog, then glided into a deep bass roll, which literally and closely resembled the roll of

distant thunder along the sky. I have heard the lion roar, but greater, deeper and more fearful is the roar of the gorilla. So deep is it that it seems to proceed less from the mouth and throat than from the deep chest and vast paunch of the beast [...]

35 His eyes began to flash fierce fire as we stood motionless on the defensive, and the crest of short hair which stands on his forehead began to twitch rapidly up and down and was perfectly frightful to look at. His powerful fangs, or enormous canines, were shown as he again sent forth a thunderous roar [...] And now truly he reminded me of nothing but some hellish dream creature — a being of that hideous order, half man half beast, which we find pictured by old artists in some representations of the infernal regions [...]

40 He advanced a few steps [...] then stopped to utter that hideous roar again — advanced again, and finally stopped when at a distance of five or six yards from us. And then as he began another of his roars and beating his breast with rage [...] I fired, and killed him.

Activity 2

1 The following student has identified that Paul Du Chaillu and his guides are nervous and frightened of the gorilla. One supporting detail for that view has been noted in the chart below. Find another four details to support this and write them down.

Du Chaillu's perspective	Supporting detail
At the beginning, he (and his guides) are nervous.	• a sharp look-out is necessary • --------------------------------- --------------------------------- • --------------------------------- --------------------------------- • --------------------------------- --------------------------------- • --------------------------------- ---------------------------------

2 Now find two further points to make about Pail Du Chaillu's perspective on encountering the gorilla and note down evidence to support them.

Du Chaillu's perspective	Supporting detail

Now re-read the opening of the 2011 article from *The Telegraph* newspaper which also describes an encounter with a gorilla.

Source B

An audience with Koko the 'talking' gorilla

She knows more than 2,000 words, has friends in high places and loves cats and old films. But in her 40th year, Koko the 'talking' gorilla seeks a new challenge – a baby

By Alex Hannaford 17 Sep 2011

5 My location is a closely guarded secret: a ranch somewhere in the Santa Cruz Mountains, several miles outside the small California town of Woodside. And for good reason, for its resident is something of a celebrity. She lives here with a male friend and both value their privacy, so much so that I'm asked to keep absolutely silent as I walk the single-track dirt path that winds through a grove of towering redwoods up to a little Portakabin.

10 Inside, I'm asked to put on a thin medical mask to cover my nose and mouth and a pair of latex gloves. Then my guide, Lorraine, tells me to follow another dirt trail to a different outbuilding. This one has a small wooden porch attached and it's here that I sit on a plastic chair and look up at an open door, separated from the outside world by a wire fence that stretches the length and width of the frame. And there she is: Koko. A 300lb
15 lowland gorilla, sitting staring back at me and pointing to an impressive set of teeth.

I'd been told beforehand not to make eye contact initially as it can be perceived as threatening, and so I glare at the ground. But I can't help stealing brief glances at this beautiful creature.

Koko, if you're not familiar, was taught American sign language when she was about a
20 year old. Now 40, she apparently has a working vocabulary of more than 1,000 signs and understands around 2,000 words of spoken English.

I sign "hello", which looks like a sailor's salute, and she emits a long, throaty growl. "Don't worry, that means she likes you," comes the disembodied voice of Dr Penny Patterson, the foundation's president and scientific director, from somewhere inside the
25 enclosure. "It's the gorilla equivalent of a purr." Koko grins at me, then turns and signs to Dr Patterson. "She wants to see your mouth… wait, she particularly wants to see your tongue," Dr Patterson says, and I happily oblige, pulling my mask down, poking my tongue out and returning the grin.

Another soft, deep roar. Dr Patterson emerges from a side door, closing it behind her, and
30 joins me on the porch. Koko makes a sign. Dr Patterson translates: "Visit. Do you."

"Oh, sweetheart," she says to Koko, then turns to me: "She'd like you to go inside."

Koko lightly takes my hand and places it in the bend in her arm before leading me around the small room, cluttered with soft toys and clothes designed to stimulate her imagination. I shuffle along the floor so as not to seem threatening, but it's amazing how gentle she is.

35 My wife and I had a baby daughter just three weeks before my visit and I pull a photo out of my pocket to show her. I've learnt the sign – pointing to myself and then making a rocking motion with my arms – to indicate "my baby". Incredibly, Koko takes the photo, looks at it, and kisses it. She then turns, picks up a doll from the mound of toys beside her and holds it up to me.

Think about the similarities and differences between the writers' attitudes towards the gorilla in Source A and Source B. Like Paul Du Chaillu, Alex Hannaford is also quite nervous ("A 300lb lowland gorilla, sitting staring back at me and pointing to an impressive set of teeth") and is approaching the gorilla silently, but his perspective is quite different to the nineteenth-century explorer and hunter. Look at the following example Question 4.

For this question, you need to refer to the **whole of Source A** together with the **whole of Source B**.

Compare how the writers convey their different views and experiences of encountering a gorilla.

In your answer, you could:

- compare their different views and experiences
- compare the methods they use to convey those views and experiences
- support your ideas with references to both texts.

Activity 3

Identify two ways in which Alex Hannaford's perspective is different and support your point with evidence.

Alex Hannaford's perspective	Evidence

Activity 4

Look back at the tables you completed in Activities 2 and 3. Take one point and supporting evidence about Paul Du Chaillu's perspective from the Source A table and compare it with a contrasting point about Alex Hannaford's perspective from your Source B table. Write a sentence to compare them using the word 'whereas' to indicate the contrast.

Demonstrating a detailed understanding

In order to achieve a high level for your response to Question 4, you need to show a detailed understanding of the different ideas and perspectives in both texts. This means that your answer must refer to a wide range of evidence for comparison. It is not enough to simply state that the writer of Source A shows the gorilla as a dangerous wild beast whereas the writer of Source B describes it as being friendly and gentle despite its strength. You must go on to analyse those views and the methods used to convey them.

Complete the following activity to explore how you can demonstrate a detailed understanding of an idea or perspective in the text.

Activity 5

Re-read Source A on page 111. As you do so, ask yourself the following questions:

- How has Du Chaillu chosen to convey his view that the gorilla is a violent, wild beast to the reader?

- How does he structure the writing to achieve this?

- How does he choose his language to achieve this?

- How does the **tone** of the writing reflect this?

Collect your ideas about the different methods Du Chaillu uses to convey his view in the following table.

Paul Du Chaillu's view: He thinks of the gorilla as a dangerous, violent wild beast.
Structure
Language
Tone

Key term

Tone: manner of expression that shows the writer's attitude, for example, an apologetic or angry tone.

Exam tip

Tone is a useful term when analysing a writer's perspective. Writers sometimes change their tone during a piece and spotting this can help you to see when there is a change of perspective.

Activity 6

Re-read Source B on page 113 and focus on the contrasting perspective:

The writer of Source B discovers that the gorilla is friendly and gentle despite her strength.

Collect your ideas about the different methods Alex Hannaford uses to convey his view in the following table.

Alex Hannaford's view: He discovers that the gorilla is friendly and gentle despite her strength.
Structure
Language
Tone

Exam tip

When answering Question 4, establish the writers' views and perspectives but then make sure that you cover a range of methods they use too. Think about structure, tone and language features, explaining how they convey the views of each writer.

Activity 7

Look back at your completed tables for Activities 5 and 6. Using the points and evidence you have collected, write a paragraph comparing how the writers convey their different views and experiences of encountering a gorilla.

Remember to compare the writers' views and experiences and the methods they use to convey these, supporting your ideas with references to both texts.

Exam tip

Of all the methods that a writer uses, structure can be the most difficult to compare. Think about the sequencing of events in the two source texts. In Source B, for instance, the writer structures the text by taking the reader through the different stages of entry to Koko's enclosure so that we gradually get closer to her. Think about what effect his choice to take us on this journey has on the reader.

Writing a perceptive comparison

In order to acieve the highest marks for Question 4 you need to compare ideas and perspectives in a perceptive way.

To do this, you need to move on from obvious comparisons and look for insights into the writers' ideas and perspectives and the methods used to convey these. These are details that a reader might not notice on first reading.

For example, in Source B the writer's perspective changes during the piece. At first he is wary of Koko because of her immense power but at the end he describes her as gentle and motherly.

Activity 8

Re-read Source B on page 113 and decide where in the text Alex Hannaford's perspective shifts. Write down the first words that indicate this change and explain the methods Hannaford uses to convey this shift in perspective.

First words: _____

_____

_____

Methods: _____

_____

_____

_____

_____

_____

Now look at an extract from Student A's answer on the opposite page to the example Question 4 below.

For this question, you need to refer to the **whole of Source A** together with the **whole of Source B**.

Compare how the writers convey their different views and experiences of encountering a gorilla.

In your answer, you could:

- compare their different views and experiences
- compare the methods they use to convey those views and experiences
- support your ideas with references to both texts.

Look closely at the annotations which indicate where the answer displays features of a Level 4 response. These annotations indicate where the answer:

shows *detailed understanding*   *analyses* methods

compares ideas *perceptively*   selects *judicious supporting detail*.

> Perceptive comparison – the student sees that both writers build suspense before revealing the gorillas

Student A

Right from the beginning, the writers describe their experiences very differently although there are some striking similarities in their methods. Both writers build suspense before they introduce the gorillas but where Du Chaillu builds the anticipation by describing the ways in which the 'natives' respond to the sound of 'someone breaking down branches or twigs of trees' so that we are expecting a violent, dangerous 'great beast' to emerge, Hannaford builds a picture in our minds of a shy 'celebrity' who doesn't want to be disturbed. He takes the reader on a journey through the various security procedures as if he is approaching a reclusive movie star. When he eventually gets to meet the Koko, Hannaford is initially nervous of her 'staring back at me and pointing to an impressive set of teeth' but it isn't long before his perception changes – 'Koko lightly takes my hand and places it in the bend in her arm'. When the scientist addresses Koko as 'sweetheart' this marks an important change in his perception of Koko, although he is still careful 'not to seem threatening'. Du Chaillu, on the other hand makes no attempt to communicate with the gorilla. He is only there to kill it, after all, rather than to communicate with it, so his focus is completely on how powerful and terrifying it is, using poetic language to strike terror into the hearts of his readers– 'glaring large deep grey eyes, and a hellish expression of face, which seemed to me like some nightmare vision', a very marked contrast to Hannaford's comment that 'it's amazing how gentle she is.'

> Methods – this is a structural method for building suspense

> Judicious supporting detail

> Judicious supporting detail

> Compares ideas perceptively

Activity 9

Can you find any other examples of the features of a Level 4 response in Student A's answer? Add your own annotations to identify these.

Note how the student uses some long, multi-clause sentences to compare both sources and provide evidence. Think about how you can use the following *discourse markers* to introduce the comparisons you make.

- Whereas
- Unlike
- Similarly
- On the other hand
- Both
- However
- Conversely
- Instead of

Activity 10

Read the source texts on pages 122 and 123 and answer the example Question 4 below. Source A is an article from *The Daily Telegraph* newspaper called "Digital learning: how technology is reshaping teaching". Source B is an extract from a letter Charles Dickens wrote to *The Daily News* newspaper in 1846 describing his visit to a 'Ragged School' – a free school for children whose families were too poor to pay for education.

For this question, you need to refer to the **whole of Source A** together with the **whole of Source B**.

Compare how the writers have conveyed their different views of schools.

In your answer, you could:

- compare their different views and descriptions
- compare the methods they use to convey those views and descriptions
- support your ideas with references to both texts.

Begin your answer here and continue on blank paper if you need to.

Activity 10 *continued*

Now that you have practised the skills needed for a higher-grade response to Question 4, complete the Progress Check activity below.

Progress check

Re-read your answer to Activity 10.

1 Use three highlighter pens of different colours to highlight sections of your response to show where you have satisfied each of the criteria for a higher-grade answer.

2 Complete the table below to assess your progress in relation to each of the Level 4 criteria.

		Yes	No
Comparing writers' ideas and perspectives	I can compare ideas and perspectives in a **perceptive** way.		
	I can show a **detailed** understanding of the different ideas and perspectives in both texts.		
How methods are used to convey ideas and perspectives	I can **analyse** how writers' methods are used.		
Supporting your ideas with appropriate textual references	I can select a **range of judicious** supporting detail from both texts.		

Source A

Digital learning: how technology is reshaping teaching

As the new school term approaches, Sophie Curtis looks at the impact technology is having in the classroom

By Sophie Curtis 23 Aug 2014

5   Not so long ago, the back to school season was marked by a dash to Woolworths for exercise books and colouring pencils. Today it's not just the shop that's gone; books and pencils are joined by Chromebook laptops and tablet computers as educational essentials [...]

Over four in 10 households now have a tablet, meaning that children are
10 becoming computer-literate before they've even started primary school – and we've all heard about the techno-babies who can handle an iPad before they have learnt how to tie their own shoelaces.

It is unsurprising, therefore, that technology is playing an increasingly central role in the classroom – not just in ICT lessons, where children
15 will start learning to write code from the age of five this year, but in English, Maths and Science lessons as well.

I recently took part in an interactive experiment run by Argos and Intel, which involved sitting through two English lessons – one the old fashioned way without any kind of technology, and the second with all
20 the latest gadgets at my disposal.

The first involved reading a scene from Shakespeare's Macbeth, listening to the teacher talk through the themes and then writing my own analysis with pen and paper. The second involved watching a series of video clips depicting differing interpretations of the balcony
25 scene from Shakespeare's Romeo and Juliet, using the internet to research the themes, and then typing my own interpretation on a laptop.

While the first lesson required intense and sustained concentration, the second was undeniably more compelling. I'm not sure I learnt any more about Romeo and Juliet than I did about Macbeth, but at no point
30 during the second lesson did I find my mind wandering, which is half the battle teachers fight every day [...]

As a pupil, I was also able to take part in quizzes and submit my answers digitally. The teacher was then able to pull up individual pupils' answers on the smartboard and show them to the rest of the class.

35 Anyone who has been through a more traditional education system may find these techniques gimmicky, but many teachers now claim that flashy multimedia lessons are the only way to engage children whose ability to absorb information has been shaped by continuous exposure to technology from a young age.

40 Using technology in an educational environment not only better reflects children's life outside the classroom, but also allows them to hone their digital skills in a way that will continue to be valuable throughout their adult life [...]

Source B

It consisted at that time of either two or three – I forget which – miserable rooms, upstairs in a miserable house. In the best of these, the pupils in the female school were being taught to read and write; and though there were among the number, many wretched creatures
5   steeped in degradation to the lips, they were tolerably quiet, and listened with apparent earnestness and patience to their instructors. The appearance of this room was sad and melancholy, of course – how could it be otherwise! – but, on the whole, encouraging.

The close, low chamber at the back, in which the boys were crowded,
10   was so foul and stifling as to be, at first, almost insupportable. But its moral aspect was so far worse than its physical, that this was soon forgotten. Huddled together on a bench about the room, and shown out by some flaring candles stuck against the walls, were a crowd of boys, varying from mere infants to young men; sellers of fruit, herbs,
15   **lucifer-matches**, flints; sleepers under the dry arches of bridges; young thieves and beggars – with nothing natural to youth about them: with nothing frank, ingenuous, or pleasant in their faces; low-browed, vicious, cunning, wicked; abandoned of all help but this; speeding downward to destruction; and UNUTTERABLY IGNORANT [...]

20   This was the Class I saw at the Ragged School. They could not be trusted with books; they could only be instructed orally; they were difficult of reduction to anything like attention, obedience, or decent behaviour; their benighted ignorance in reference to the Deity, or to any social duty (how could they guess at any social duty, being so
25   discarded by all social teachers but the gaoler and the hangman!) was terrible to see. Yet, even here, and among these, something had been done already. The Ragged School was of recent date and very poor; but he had inculcated some association with the name of the Almighty, which was not an oath, and had taught them to look
30   forward in a hymn (they sang it) to another life, which would correct the miseries and woes of this.

Glossary

lucifer-matches
  – lucifer-matches were the first cheap safety matches

Overview of the Writing section

The writing section of Paper 2 is worth 40 marks, the same as the reading section. You should expect to spend about 45 minutes on your writing, splitting your writing into three stages:

- planning (5–10 minutes)
- writing (30–35 minutes)
- checking, proofreading and making final improvements (5 minutes).

You will be given a single task, linked in a general way to the topic of the two texts that you compared in Section A. You will not need to use any of the content from the source texts you have read, although you may if you think that it is relevant.

The task will ask you to express your own views about a topic, writing for a specific purpose and audience (for example, for a school magazine). Usually, these prompts will encourage you to write at length for a general reader using Standard English.

How your writing will be marked

Your writing will be marked against two Assessment Objectives:

Assessment Objective	The writing skills that you need to demonstrate
AO5 (Content and organization)	Communicate clearly, effectively and imaginatively, selecting and adapting tone, style and register for different forms, purposes and audiences.
	Organize information and ideas, using structural and grammatical features to support coherence and cohesion of texts.
AO6 (Technical accuracy)	Use a range of vocabulary and sentence structures for clarity, purpose and effect, with accurate spelling and punctuation.

Overall, the writing question in Paper 1 is worth a maximum of 40 marks: 24 marks are available for content and organization (AO5); 16 marks are available for technical accuracy (AO6).

The writing task

Expressing your own point of view

In Section B of Paper 2, the writing task is likely to present you with:

- an **assertion**, for example, 'Homework has no value'

and/or

- a statement of opinion, for example, 'Festivals and fairs should be banned. They encourage bad behaviour and are disruptive to local communities.'

You will then be asked to write an article for a specified publication either for or against the assertion or statement. Although the audience for your writing is likely to be specified, in most cases it should be interpreted as being for a general reader. This means that you should use Standard English with correct grammar, punctuation and spelling.

To produce a higher-grade response to the writing task you will need to do the following.

Content

- ☐ Make sure the register you use to present your viewpoint is convincing and compelling for your audience – for instance, aim to manipulate your readers through appealing to their emotions or ethics. How will you convey your viewpoint to *all* your readers, not just people like you?

- ☐ Ensure that the tone, style and register of your writing is assuredly matched to your purpose – for instance, if your piece is humorous or angry, do your language choices reflect this?

- ☐ Craft your writing, using precise, sophisticated vocabulary and linguistic devices (such as figurative language to bring your writing to life or choosing vocabulary that reflects the tone of your writing).

Organization

- ☐ Incorporate varied and effective structural features – for instance, incorporating anecdotes from your own experience or quotations to support your ideas.

- ☐ Incorporate a range of complex and convincing ideas to make your writing compelling – for instance, starting with a description of a scene which illustrates the point you are going to make and then going on to argue your point.

- ☐ Construct fluently linked paragraphs with seamlessly integrated discourse markers.

Technical accuracy

☐ Consistently demarcate your sentences securely and accurately.

☐ Use a wide range of punctuation with a high level of accuracy.

☐ Use a full range of appropriate sentence forms for effect.

☐ Use Standard English consistently and appropriately with secure control of complex grammatical structures.

☐ Achieve a high level of accuracy in spelling, including ambitious vocabulary.

☐ Use extensive and ambitious vocabulary.

Look back at your writing skills self-evaluation on pages 8–9 and tick the skills that you need to prioritize to achieve a higher grade.

Planning your writing

The writing task in Section B will provide an assertion or statement to act as a stimulus for your writing, so use this to help you to develop your ideas as you plan.

> 'Smartphones are distracting. They should be banned from all schools and colleges.'
>
> Write an article for a parents' newsletter in which you either agree or disagree with this view.

Exam tip

Very often simply agreeing with the assertion is limiting because it doesn't give you as many opportunities to make more sophisticated arguments.

Student A has decided to disagree with the assertion and started to plan their response to the writing task:

Student A

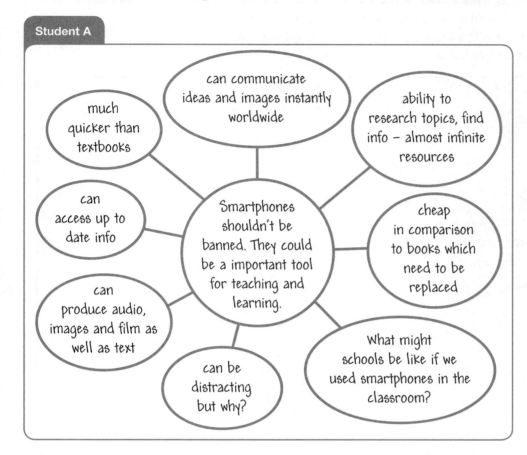

- much quicker than textbooks
- can communicate ideas and images instantly worldwide
- ability to research topics, find info – almost infinite resources
- can access up to date info
- Smartphones shouldn't be banned. They could be a important tool for teaching and learning.
- cheap in comparison to books which need to be replaced
- can produce audio, images and film as well as text
- can be distracting but why?
- What might schools be like if we used smartphones in the classroom?

Exam tip

Using a spider diagram can help you to generate and organize ideas for your writing. Try generating questions as well as statements, as answering these will help you to come up with more ideas that you might otherwise have missed.

You can see from the plan that Student A has thought of two further questions to address in her writing:

1 Why can smartphones be distracting? The student has realised that she must deal with the statement in the question. It's undeniable that smartphones can be distracting in traditional classrooms. How can this be overcome?

2 What might schools be like if we used smartphones in the classroom? Here, the student has seen an opportunity to write about how learning might look in the future. Might classrooms be quite different if we started using smartphones as tools for learning?

Both of these questions offer Student A the opportunity to make more complex arguments to develop the following point of view:

- Smartphones should not only be allowed in schools but that their use should be actively encouraged for educational purposes and that they needn't be distracting if they are used in this way.

Activity 1

Add your own ideas to the spider diagrams below. Remember the points you make should help to develop more sophisticated, complex arguments, supporting Student A's point of view.

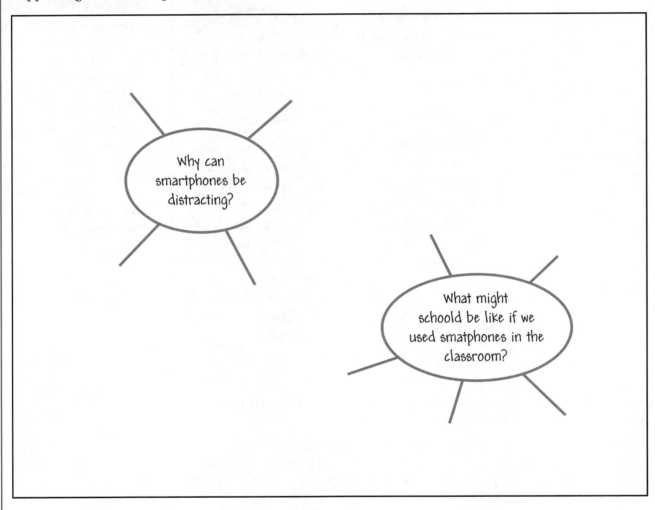

Remember to keep the purpose, audience and form for your writing in mind during the planning stage. In this task, you have been asked to write an article for a parents' newsletter. When you have completed your plan ask yourself:

• Have I included points which will appeal to my audience?

• Does my plan satisfy the purpose of the task?

Activity 2

1 Look back at the spider diagrams on page 127 and above. Highlight any points that you think would be particularly relevant to the target audience of parents.

2 Add any other points to the spider diagrams that you think would appeal to this audience.

Structuring your writing

Once you have generated your ideas, you need to think about the way you organize these in order to construct a compelling piece of writing. An effective structure is crucial if you want to gain the highest marks in this task.

A helpful way to think about the structure of your writing is to decide how you want to guide your reader through your ideas to reach your conclusion. An effective structure will make your views appear more convincing and compelling.

When planning the structure of your writing, you should consider:

- how you can create an engaging opening to draw your readers in

- how you will group your ideas into fluently linked paragraphs

- the most effective order in which to present your ideas

- how you can use a variety of structural features to support the **coherence and cohesion** of your writing.

> **Key term**
>
> **Coherence and cohesion:**
> the way that a piece of writing links together in terms of vocabulary, phrases, clauses, sentences and paragraphs.

Activity 3

Look at the following points taken from the spider diagram on page 127:

☐ Smartphones can access up-to-date information.

☐ Can produce audio, images and film as well as text.

☐ Much quicker than textbooks to find information.

☐ Can communicate instantly.

☐ Can research topics and find information on anything.

☐ Cheap compared to textbooks which have to be regularly replaced.

Number the above bullet points to indicate the most effective order in which to present these ideas. Think about the links between different ideas. Discuss the reasons for your choices.

Look at how Student A has decided to structure the ideas from the spider diagram on page 127 to produce the following plan. Her notes have been expanded to make them understandable.

Student A

1   Introduction. A vision of a classroom of the future. A geography lesson. Students using their own smartphones and mini tablets. Instant information at students' and teacher's fingertips. Using software to access online videos, viewing images from around the world. Video-conferencing with students in a foreign country. Students publishing their work online to be shared instantly.

2   Back to a normal school now. Rows of desks. Tatty, out-of-date textbooks, everyone staring at one whiteboard, no talking. Very few reference books. Students laboriously handwriting their work. Limited access to the Internet (only through teacher's computer or cumbersome PC). Exaggerate for humour – leaky pens, environmentally damaging use of paper.

3   Why are students still working in this way? Address target audience: parents. If you work in an office now you don't write by hand. *You* might use video-conferencing, Skype, email, instant messaging. If *you* want to find information, you Google it. How are we preparing young people for the world of work?

4   All this is available in every teenager's pocket. Why ban the technology that we all use now and will use more in the future? Explain all its advantages. Use powerful image – a visiting alien would be confused by the fact that the students have all this technology in their pockets but don't use it.

5   Of course smartphones can be distracting. Only if they are perceived as toys not tools for learning.

6   Conclusion. Back to the vision of the future. This could all be destroyed because schools want to ban smartphone technology.

Exam tip

Although the Section B task in the exam will not ask you for a title for your writing, it can often be a good idea to think of one. A good title can help you encapsulate your point of view on the topic and writing this down can remind you to keep your writing relevant and effective.

Activity 4

Look at the following example writing task.

> 'Many young people feel that they don't have enough say in the way that the country is run. At the next election, sixteen year olds should be able to vote.'
>
> Write an article for a student newspaper in which you agree or disagree with this view.

Create a plan for your response to this writing task. You can create a spider diagram to generate ideas and then a plan like the one on page 130 to structure these ideas. Remember you need to:

- create a compelling structure, fluently linking ideas

- include any structural features in your notes, for example, addressing your reader directly

- use description and imagination to illustrate your points.

Exam tip

In Section B of the exam, one of the greatest dangers is that you run out of ideas and end up repeating yourself. To avoid this, think about your conclusion right from the start so that you have something to aim at as you write.

Writing your response

Tone, style and register

When writing your response in the exam, it is crucially important to create an engaging opening. This is where you establish the **tone**, **style** and register of your writing.

Read the following extract from the opening of a newspaper article written by the sociologist Frank Furedi. Here he expresses his view that children are no longer given the freedom to develop their independence and starts the article by describing his own childhood. As you read consider the tone, style and register that Furedi has adopted in this article.

Accidents should happen

WHEN I was a child, I loved the day the clocks went forward – it meant evenings would be lighter, giving us more time to play outside after school. It also meant that warmer weather would be on the way and that meant that my friends and I could escape from under our parents' feet and have fun or, as they saw it, get up to mischief.

Like **The Fast Show's Ron Manager**, we all remember jumpers for goalposts. But school ties came in handy, too, being used for binding the hands of boys "taken prisoner" in play raids. School shirts were stained green from lying on grass. By the time the Easter holidays came, we were never at home. We were far too busy lugging perilously large objects into trees and bushes to make "camps", from which we could launch attacks on other children.

These days, it's rare for children to spend time like this, without the company of adults, making and breaking their own rules in their own games. Today, we worry that, left unsupervised, children will fall victim to all manner of risks it is our duty to prevent. The obsession with child safety is so dominant that even the sources of spontaneous outdoor fun of a decade ago are being taken away.

Key terms

Tone: manner of expression that shows the writer's attitude, for example, an apologetic or angry tone.

Style: the language choices a writer makes, for example, using particularly figurative language.

Glossary

The Fast Show's Ron Manager – a character in the BBC TV comedy *The Fast Show* who parodied football commentators by spouting nonsense, often about the good old days of his childhood

Activity 5

1 How would you describe the tone of Frank Furedi's article?

2 How and where does the tone change?

3 Which words and phrases (stylistic choices) contribute most strongly to his argument and why?

Look again at Student A's plan for the opening of their article:

Student A

1 Introduction. A vision of a classroom of the future. A geography lesson. Students using their own smartphones and mini tablets. Instant information at students' and teacher's fingertips. Using software to access online videos, viewing images from around the world. Video-conferencing with students in a foreign country. Students publishing their work online to be shared instantly.

2 Back to a normal school now. Rows of desks. Tatty, out-of-date textbooks, everyone staring at one whiteboard, no talking. Very few reference books. Students laboriously handwriting their work. Limited access to the Internet (only through teacher's computer or cumbersome PC). Exaggerate for humour – leaky pens, environmentally damaging use of paper.

Activity 6

1 Write an opening paragraph based on point 1 of these notes in which you conjure up a positive vision of a classroom which uses modern smartphone technology to enhance learning. Write in the present tense and think about the choices you make to create an appropriate tone, style and register for your writing in a similar way to Furedi. You could use the suggested opening phrase:

I want to take you to visit a classroom...

2 Now write the second paragraph of your article. This should address point 2 of the plan – the actual classroom of today in which smartphones are banned. Aim to contrast it with the previous paragraph, as Furedi does. Think about an effective sentence to start your second paragraph which links it to your first.

3 Look back at the paragraphs you have written and highlight:
- any words or phrases that help establish a positive and enthusiastic tone in the first paragraph
- any words or phrases that help establish a dull and depressing tone in the second paragraph
- where you think the structure of your opening is effective in manipulating the reader to agree with your point of view.

Crafting your opening

You can use a range of approaches to open your writing, depending on the purpose, audience and form of the writing task you are completing. Look at the different examples below and think about the tone and style used in each one.

A personal anecdote

I was walking towards my lesson the other day when my phone rang. This is a rare occurrence so I thought it must be important. I took it out of my pocket and just had enough time to notice that it was my mum ringing when I heard my name being shouted. Mr Jones, the scariest deputy Head was striding down the corridor towards me, his hand outstretched, ready to take my phone.

An arresting fact or piece of information

It's an astounding fact that the average teenager these days carries around in their pocket more processing power than NASA used to launch a rocket to the moon.

A rhetorical question

When was the last time you left home without your phone? If you did, I'll bet it was an accident and you felt as if you'd lost a limb.

A clichéd opinion used sarcastically

Of course, all members of the older generation know that every teenager is obsessed by their phone. We walk around all day with our eyes focused on the screen while our thumbs skitter across the glass with frightening agility, sending unsuitable texts to our friends.

> **Exam tip**
>
> If you decide to use a personal anecdote, remember this doesn't have to be true. The most important thing is that the anecdote you choose helps to illustrate your point of view.

Activity 7

Look back at the plan you made for the writing task in Activity 4 on page 131.

> 'Many young people feel that they don't have enough say in the way that the country is run. At the next election, sixteen year olds should be able to vote.'
>
> Write an article for a student newspaper in which you agree or disagree with this view.

Write the opening sentences of your article, using one of the above approaches.

Communicating your ideas in a convincing and compelling way

Once you have written an engaging opening that establishes the tone, style and register of your writing, you need to communicate your ideas in a convincing and compelling way throughout in order to achieve the highest grades. Think about the way you sequence the different arguments you make to support your point of view.

Activity 8

Complete the first draft of the article you began in Activity 7.

Structural features

In order to achieve the highest grade, you need to demonstrate a varied and inventive use of structural features in your writing. Look at the following different examples below and think about how you can use these to make your writing flow.

Integrated discourse markers

Discourse markers are words and phrases that writers use to guide readers from one point to another. To make your writing seamless and fluent you need to have a wide repertoire of these at your disposal.

Re-read the opening extract of the newspaper article about the excessive control of children's play on page 132. Now read the next few paragraphs of the article below. As you read, note how each paragraph introduces more examples but begins with a different discourse marker.

Notice how Furedi links his paragraphs with integrated discourse markers that don't disrupt the flow (unlike stand-alone discourse markers such as 'Firstly', 'moreover' or 'furthermore'). Within the paragraphs, he guides his reader through the evidence so that it is integrated into his argument.

> **Take something as apparently harmless as conkers**, a game that has probably been an accepted part of children's play since the invention of string. Well, possibly not for much longer.
>
> 5 **I recently learnt that** some local authorities were so worried that they might be sued by parents of children injured conkering that they had implemented a policy of "tree management" to make horse-chestnut trees less accessible to children.
>
> **And it gets worse. A recently published survey** by Sarah Thomson, a researcher at Keele University, **indicates that** it is
> 10 not just local authorities that are out to ban conkering. Schools, too, are banning such traditional playtime games because head teachers are anxious about being sued by litigious parents.
> **Thomson claims that** some schools have banned conkers because they fear a chestnut on a string could be used as an
> 15 "offensive weapon".

Activity 9

Look back at the first draft of the article you completed in Activity 8 on page 137. Think about how you can integrate the following discourse markers into your writing to build up evidence and present ideas supporting your point of view.

- In my experience…
- It's is undeniable that…
- Whilst I agree that… it is nevertheless the case that…
- It is clear to me that…

- As a consequence…
- It may seem that… but…
- It is generally agreed that…
- You only have to look at….
- Take, for example, …

Reference chains

Reference chains allow you to refer to or sum up a previous idea without repeating it. Read the following examples from Student B's response to whether smartphones should be allowed in class:

It is ridiculous that today's students are forbidden to use the kind of technology that their parents use every day at work.

This glaring inconsistency…

If this is the way that we educate our young people, then…

The current ludicrous state of affairs…

Note how each noun phrase refers back to the original point without having to re-state it. This enables the writer to link paragraphs together without obvious markers. Reference chains should be used within paragraphs as well, to prevent repetition and enable points to be referred to and summed up.

Key term

Reference chains: different words or phrases used to refer to the same idea, person or thing many times in a piece of writing, like links in a chain.

Activity 10

1   Read Student C's paragraph below. The lack of reference chains makes it sound clumsy and disjointed. Re-write the paragraph using reference chains to avoid repetition.

> **Student C**
>
> Most teenagers' pockets now carry more computing power than NASA used to send astronauts to the moon. Why do so many schools prevent students from using the computing power that they have? It would seem very strange to a visiting alien to see students huddled over tatty textbooks when they have all that computing power in their pockets and bags.

2   Look again at the first draft of the article you completed in Activity 8 on page 135 and check that you have used effective reference chains. Revise your writing to ensure you have demonstrated a varied and inventive use of structural features.

Vocabulary and linguistic devices

To achieve a higher grade, you need to craft your writing to make it as engaging and persuasive as possible. To do this you will need to include:

- extensive and ambitious vocabulary to communicate your point of view
- linguistic devices to create deliberate effects
- a full range of sentence forms for effect
- a wide range of punctuation, used accurately.

Re-read the following extract from Frank Furedi's article about the excessive control of children's play. The annotations highlight the different language features used and how these convey Furedi's point of view and influence the reader.

This indicates that an example is going to be provided. It addresses the reader directly by using an imperative verb.

Use of hyperbole to indicate how familiar we all are with the game.

'Conkering' is consciously humorous which sounds silly when set next to the word 'injured'.

Links with 'threatened' to form a violent image.

Use of alliteration gives this a jolly sound.

Another violent image using ambitious vocabulary. They are being sent away indoors.

Violent word carefully chosen.

Use of three adjectives – all beginning with 's'.

The word 'apparently' prepares us for what is to follow. It is used mockingly. We sensible people might think that conkering is harmless but there are some mad council officials who don't.

Short sentence. This is intended to shock us. Our familiar way of life is being taken away from us. The 'well' adds a conversational tone.

Purposely mocking the tone of local authority documents.

Again mocking the official language, this time in quotes to imply that it is a pompous phrase to describe chopping down trees.

Figurative use of 'wave' makes it sound like a destructive force.

Violent word carefully chosen.

Contrasts with the threat of the last sentence.

Links with 'threatened' to form a violent image.

A chatty interjection assumes that the reader agrees.

Use of numbers to add credibility and make the point stronger.

> Take something as apparently harmless as conkers, a game that has probably been an accepted part of children's play since the invention of string. Well, possibly not for much longer. I recently learnt that some local authorities were so worried that they might be sued by parents of children injured conkering that they had implemented a policy of "tree management" to make horse-chestnut trees less accessible to children.
>
> It is not only the school playground that has become a focus of the obsession with child safety. A wave of anxiety about children's safety outdoors threatens to turn the traditional public playground (the "rec") into an endangered species. Much-loved fixtures such as monkey bars and merry-go-rounds are soon to be consigned to the museum. Fixed goalposts are being removed. Witches' hats and the plank swing have been banished. New roundabouts are smaller and slower and, of course, the swings are shorter. One accident in a playground can lead to the permanent closure of an amenity. In Greenwich, south London, five playgrounds were shut following an incident in which a single child was injured.

Links with previous number.

Number again. Emphasizes that one accident can prevent everyone else from having fun.

Activity 11

Remind yourself of the writing task from Activity 4 on page 131:

'Many young people feel that they don't have enough say in the way that the country is run. At the next election, sixteen year olds should be able to vote.'

Write an article for a student newspaper in which you agree or disagree with this view.

Read the following paragraph from Student D's response to this task. As it stands, this response is likely to achieve a Level 3.

Student D

It is ridiculous that at sixteen you are allowed to marry and to join the army but you are not allowed to vote. If we are considered mature enough to get married or join the army, then we should have a say in how our country is run. In the nineteenth century, women were once denied the vote. In the future people will look back and be amazed at how we denied our young people the opportunity to take part in the democratic process.

Rewrite this paragraph so that it includes:

- extensive and ambitious vocabulary to communicate the point of view
- linguistic devices to create deliberate effects
- a full range of sentence forms for effect
- a wide range of punctuation, used accurately.

You can extend the paragraph, introducing new content if necessary, in order to communicate the ideas in a convincing and compelling way.

Activity 12

1 Look again at the first draft of the article you completed in Activity 8 on page 135. Read through each paragraph carefully, looking for opportunities to include ambitious vocabulary, linguistic devices and sentence forms to create deliberate effects.

2 Rewrite any paragraphs that you think could be improved.

Crafting your writing

Remember in the exam you will only have 45 minutes to plan, write and proofread your work, unlike a professional writer who might have taken a day or more to craft their writing. To give yourself the best chance of achieving the highest grade for your writing in Section B of Paper 2, you need to practise using a range of language features when writing for different audiences and purposes, and in different forms.

Look back over any writing tasks you have done and use the following chart to identify which language features you have used. Against each language feature, give yourself a rating from 1 -5 with 1 being 'I hardly ever use this' and 5 being 'I feel confident using this'. Add any other language features you identify to the chart.

Language feature	Rating
Hyperbole and humorous exaggeration	
Carefully chosen linked vocabulary to achieve an effect	
Ambitious vocabulary (more unusual but carefully chosen words)	
Creative use of punctuation (e.g. quotation marks to denote mockery or exclamation marks to denote anger)	
Conversational 'chatty' tone used sparingly for effect	
Figurative language techniques such as metaphor, simile or alliteration	
Varied sentence forms for effect	
Lists used for emphasis (usually three examples)	

> **Key term**
>
> **Hyperbole:** the use of exaggeration as a rhetorical device or figure of speech. It can be very useful if you want to ridicule your opponents' views (e.g. Our Deputy Head, Mr. Jones whose sole purpose in life seemed to be to rid the world of smartphones).

Any features that you gave a rating of 3 or lower for should be the focus of your revision and practice.

> **Exam tip**
>
> Furedi uses ironic quotation marks to mock what he sees as the ridiculous language of his opponents (e.g. 'tree management'). This can be a powerful weapon to use in your own writing.

Technical accuracy

In Section B of Paper 2, you will be awarded up to 24 marks for AO5 (composition and organization) but don't forget there are 16 marks available for AO6 (technical accuracy). To ensure that you gain as many marks for AO6 as possible, make sure that you:

- re-read your writing as you go and leave enough time for a final proofread at the end
- remember to check that you have used a wide range of punctuation accurately
- use a range of sophisticated vocabulary
- use a range of sentence forms for effect.

Sentence forms

To achieve Level 4, you will need to use a range of sentence forms including single and multi-clause sentences. Before you go on to practise a range of different forms, carry out the following self-assessment of your writing.

Activity 13

1 Re-read any extended writing that you have completed in this book and look for the following:

1 Any sentence with a single comma and more than one verb	
2 Any sentence with two commas and more than one verb	
3 Any sentence that includes a semi-colon or a dash and two verbs	

2 Mark each one in the margin with a different colour. Add up the numbers of each. You should find that you have a large number of examples of 1, a smaller number of examples of 2 and a few examples of 3. If you have less than half your sentences highlighted, then you need to work on your sentence forms to develop their complexity.

The choices you make when constructing a sentence can change the effect it creates. For example, adverbs (for example, 'finally', 'unfortunately') and adverbial phrases (for example, 'despite all our efforts', 'on the other hand') can be moved around within a sentence to change its emphasis and rhythm.

Look at the following example:

Young people are <u>unfairly</u> prevented from casting their votes.

<u>Unfairly</u>, young people are prevented from casting their votes.

Both sentences are clear and effective but moving the adverb subtly changes the emphasis. In the first sentence, putting '*unfairly*' next to '*prevented*' links the two words and puts the emphasis on '*prevented*'. In the second sentence, the position of '*unfairly*' at the front makes it apply to the whole of the rest of the sentence.

Activity 14

1 Experiment with the adverbials in different positions in the following sentences to see how the emphasis can be changed. As you write each sentence, read it aloud to hear how different each version sounds. Remember to use commas where necessary.

Sentence	Adverbial (or adverb)
All young people should be taught about politics and our democratic system.	as a matter of course
Teenagers are perceived as being immature.	often
This may cause young people to lose interest in politics.	unfortunately

2 Look again at the first draft of the article you completed in Activity 8 on page 135. Identify any adverbials you have used and experiment with moving these to improve the effectiveness of your sentences.

In formal academic English, writers use a lot of abstract nouns and noun phrases instead of verbs. This is called **nominalization** and can give the writing a more sophisticated and academic style. Look at the following sentence from Frank Furedi's article with examples of nominalization underlined.

The obsession with child safety is so dominant that even the sources of spontaneous outdoor fun of a decade ago are being taken away.

Here is how nominalization can change a sentence to clarify it and make it sound more sophisticated:

If young people were involved in voting in elections, they would...

becomes

The involvement of young people in the democratic process would...

This is achieved by turning the verb 'were involved' into the noun 'involvement' and 'voting in elections' becomes 'the democratic process'.

Key term

Nominalization: changing a verb into noun to create a more sophisticated, academic style.

Activity 15

1 Read through your own writing to find a sentence which could be improved through nominalization. Write the original sentence and then the improved version.

Original sentence: _____
_____
_____
_____
_____
_____

Sentence with nominalization: _____
_____
_____
_____
_____
_____

2 Look again at the first draft of the article you completed in Activity 8 on page 135. Can you find any opportunities to nominalize?

Think about how you combine the different sentence forms you use to build effective paragraphs. Many of your paragraphs are likely to start with a topic sentence (which introduces the content) followed by supporting ideas (evidence and examples).

Activity 16

Look at the following ideas about why children's play should not be restricted:

- Restricting children's play stifles their initiative.

- When children's play is supervised it is not really play.

- Restricting how children play stifles their desire to be adventurous. Children need to play on their own.

- Unsupervised activities are crucial to help children develop.

- Children can't learn to make decisions if they are being supervised.

- Children have to learn to make decisions for themselves.

1   Use the ideas in the bullet points to write a paragraph which includes a variety of sentence forms. You can change the order of the ideas and add as many words as you like to link the ideas. You should include:

- multi–clause sentences
- single-clause sentences
- nominalization.

---

2   Compare your paragraph to Frank Furedi's original paragraph below. Note how each sentence performs a different function and is formed accordingly. How close is it to your version?

> This restrictive approach towards play stifles children's initiative and desire for adventure. Supervised play is virtual play. Children need to play on their own – unsupervised activities are crucial for their development. For children to become responsible, they have to learn to make decisions for themselves, something they can never do under a parent's watchful eye.

Exam tip

To achieve Level 4 you must use a wide range of sentence forms including multi-clause sentences designed to convey complex information. This means you need to know how to use commas, semi-colons and dashes. Practise reading some of your more complex sentences aloud to check that the punctuation is effective.

45
minutes

Activity 17

Now that you have practised your writing skills, it's time to put them all together as you write a complete response to an example Paper 2 Section B writing task.

> 'Young people today are too vain, always taking "selfies" and worrying about their appearance. This is a sign that society is becoming more self-obsessed and shallow.'
>
> Write an article for a national newspaper in which you express your views on this topic.

Remember to use your time carefully, dividing it between planning, writing and proofreading your work. For example:

- planning (5–10 minutes)
- writing (30–35 minutes)
- checking, proofreading and making final improvements (5 minutes).

Start your writing below and continue on blank paper.

Exam tip

One of the most important qualities of a high-level response for this part of the paper is that your views are convincing enough to make an impression on your reader. As you write, ask yourself whether you have expressed each element of your viewpoint as powerfully as possible. Have you used:

- compelling content?
- convincing examples?
- the most effective language?
- powerful rhetorical devices?
- varied and effective discourse markers to structure your writing?

Progress check

Now that you have practised the skills needed for a higher-grade response to a Paper 2 Section B writing task, carry out the progress check below. Use three highlighter pens of different colours to highlight passages of your answer to Activity 17 to show where you have satisfied each of the criteria for a higher grade.

Paper/AO	Skills	Basic skills descriptors	Check ✔	Target higher grade skills descriptors	Check ✔
Paper 2 AO5	Communicate clearly, effectively and imaginatively.	I can communicate my ideas successfully most of the time.		I can communicate my ideas convincingly, affecting the reader's response.	
	Select and adapt tone, style and register.	I have some control of the tone, style and register of my writing and they are usually appropriate.		I am confident in adopting and sustaining an appropriate tone, style and register for my writing to achieve subtle effects.	
		I can use a variety of vocabulary and some linguistic devices in my writing.		I can use an extensive and ambitious vocabulary, and a consciously crafted range of linguistic devices to achieve effects.	
Paper 2 AO5	Organize ideas.	I have a variety of relevant ideas in my writing and can make links between them.		I can develop and integrate complex and engaging ideas in my writing.	
	Use structural and grammatical features.	I can use paragraphs to organize my writing and sometimes use discourse markers.		I can link paragraphs coherently and consistently using integrated discourse markers.	
		I can use some structural features in my writing.		I can use a variety of effective structural features.	

 # My target skills

List any AO5 skills you need to improve the reach the higher grade skills descriptors.

1 ---

2 ---

3 ---

4 ---

5 ---

Use this self-evaluation to help you to plan your work, so that you spend most of your time targeting the skills that you most need to develop.

Paper/AO	Skills	Basic skills descriptors	Check ✔	Target higher grade skills descriptors	Check ✔
Paper 1 AO6	Demarcation and punctuation	I usually write in full sentences and can use full stops and capital letters accurately.		I consistently use a range of punctuation to demarcate my sentences accurately.	
		I can use some punctuation marks, e.g. question marks and speech marks.		I can use a wide range of punctuation with a very high level of accuracy.	
	Sentence forms and Standard English	I can sometimes use different sentence forms in my writing, e.g. rhetorical questions.		I can use a full range of sentence forms in my writing to achieve specific effects on the reader.	
		I usually write sentences which are grammatically correct and can use some Standard English.		I can write and control sentences with complex grammatical structures and consistently use Standard English.	
	Spelling and vocabulary	I can spell basic words and some more complex words accurately.		I can spell most words accurately, including more ambitious words.	
		I can use a variety of vocabulary, including some complex words.		I can use an extensive and ambitious range of vocabulary.	

My target skills

List any AO6 skills you need to improve the reach the higher grade skills descriptors.

1 -

2 -

3 -

4 -

5 -

Use this self-evaluation to help you to plan your work, so that you spend most of your time targeting the skills that you most need to develop.

Sample Paper 1

Source A:

This extract is from the novel The Bees *by Laline Paull. The novel is set in a beehive and in this extract the writer describes Flora 717, a worker bee, being born.*

The cell squeezed her and the air was hot and fetid. All the joints of her body burned from her frantic twisting against the walls, her head was pressed into her chest and her legs shot with cramp, but her struggles had worked–one wall felt weaker. She kicked out with all her strength and felt something crack and break. She forced and tore and bit until there was a jagged hole into fresher air beyond. 5

She dragged her body through and fell out onto the floor of an alien world. Static roared through her brain, thunderous vibration shook the ground and a thousand scents dazed her. All she could do was breathe until gradually the vibration and static subsided and the scent evaporated into the air. Her rigid body unlocked and she calmed as knowledge filled her mind. 10

This was the Arrivals Hall and she was a worker. Her kin was Flora and her number was 717. Certain of her first task, she set about cleaning out her cell. In her violent struggle to hatch she had broken the whole front wall, unlike her neater neighbours. She looked, then followed their example, piling her debris neatly by the ruins. The activity cleared her senses and she felt the vastness of the Arrivals Hall, and how the vibrations in the air changed in different areas. 15

Row upon row of cells like hers stretched into the distance, and there the cells were quiet but resonant as if the occupants still slept. Immediately around her was great activity with many recently broken and cleared-out chambers, and many more cracking and falling as new bees arrived. The differing scents of her neighbours also came into focus, some sweeter, some sharper, all of them pleasant to absorb. 20

With a hard erratic pulse in the ground, a young female came running down the corridor between the cells, her face frantic.

'Halt!' Harsh voices reverberated from both ends of the corridor and a strong astringent scent rose in the air. Every bee stopped moving but the young bee stumbled and fell across Flora's pile of debris. Then she clawed her way into the remains of the broken cell and huddled in the corner, her little hands up. 25

Cloaked in a bitter scent which hid their faces and made them identical, the dark figures strode down the corridor towards Flora. Pushing her aside, they dragged out the weeping young bee. At the sight of their spiked gauntlets, a spasm of fear in Flora's brain released more knowledge. 30

They were police.

'You fled inspection.' One of them pulled at the girl's wings, while another examined the four still-wet membranes. The edge of one was shrivelled.

'Spare me,' she cried. 'I will not fly, I will serve in any other way—' 35

'Deformity is evil. Deformity is not permitted.'

Before the bee could speak the two officers pressed her head down until there was a sharp crack. She hung limp between them and they dropped her body in the corridor.

'You.' A peculiar rasping voice addressed Flora and she did not know which one spoke, but stared at the black hooks on the backs of their legs. 'Hold still.' Long black callipers slid from their gauntlets and they measured her height. 'Excessive variation. Abnormal.' 40

'That will be all, officers.' At the kind voice and fragrant smell, the police released Flora. They bowed to a tall and well-groomed bee with a beautiful face.

'Sister Sage, this one is obscenely ugly.'

'And excessively large.'

'It would appear so. Thank you, officers, you may go.' 45

Sister Sage waited for them to leave. She smiled at Flora.

'To fear them is good. Be still while I read your kin—'

'I am Flora 717.'

Sister Sage raised her antennae. 'A sanitation worker who speaks. Most notable …'

Flora stared at her tawny and gold face with its huge dark eyes. 'Am I to be killed?' 50

Section A: Reading

Answer **all** questions in this section.

You are advised to spend about 45 minutes on this section.

---

0 1 Read the first paragraph of the source, lines 1–5.

List **four** things from this part of the text about Flora's experience of hatching. **[4 marks]**

A _____

_____

B _____

_____

C _____

_____

D _____

_____

0 2 Look in detail at this extract from lines 6–16 of the source.

> She dragged her body through and fell out onto the floor of an alien world. Static roared through her brain, thunderous vibration shook the ground and a thousand scents dazed her. All she could do was breathe until gradually the vibration and static subsided and the scent evaporated into the air. Her rigid body unlocked and she calmed as knowledge filled her mind.
>
> This was the Arrivals Hall and she was a worker. Her kin was Flora and her number was 717. Certain of her first task, she set about cleaning out her cell. In her violent struggle to hatch she had broken the whole front wall, unlike her neater neighbours. She looked, then followed their example, piling her debris neatly by the ruins. The activity cleared her senses and she felt the vastness of the Arrivals Hall, and how the vibrations in the air changed in different areas.

How does the writer use language to describe Flora's first experience of the world of the hive?

You could include the writer's choice of:

- words and phrases
- language features and techniques
- sentence forms.   **[8 marks]**

0 3 You now need to think about the **whole** of the **source**.

This text is from the opening of a novel.

How has the writer structured the text to interest you as a reader?

You could write about:

- what the writer focuses your attention on at the beginning
- how and why the writer changes this focus as the source develops
- any other structural features that interest you.   **[8 marks]**

0 4 Focus this part of your answer on the second part of the source, **from line 20 to the end**.

A student, having read this section of the text, said: 'This part of the text, from when the police arrive, shows how violent and controlled bee society is. You really feel frightened for Flora until Sister Sage saves her.'

To what extent do you agree?

In your response, you could:

- consider your own impressions of bee society
- evaluate how the writer has created these impressions
- support your opinions with references to the text.   **[20 marks]**

Section B: Writing

You are advised to spend about 45 minutes on this section.

Write in full sentences.

You are reminded of the need to plan your answer.

You should leave enough time to check your work at the end

| 0 5 | You have been asked to contribute to a new creative magazine for young people.

Either: write a description suggested by this picture

Or:

Write the opening part of a story in which your main character is threatened
or bullied for being different.

(24 marks for content and organization
16 marks for technical accuracy)
[40 marks]

Sample Paper 2

Source A:

Forty years since the first picture of earth from space

Earthrise, December 1968 – the first picture of our world taken from space was published 40 years ago this week and still retains its haunting power

BY STEVE CONNOR, SCIENCE EDITOR   Saturday 10 January 2009

They went to the Moon, but ended up discovering the Earth. The crew of Apollo 8 were the first people to leave Earth's orbit and pass behind the far side of the Moon. They had been drilled and trained for just about every eventuality, save one – the awe-inspiring sight of seeing our own planet hanging over an empty lunar horizon.

It later became known as "Earthrise" and the image of the world rising in the dark vastness   5
of space over a sun-lit lunar landscape became an iconic reminder of our lonely planet's splendid isolation and delicate fragility.

The image was captured during Christmas Eve 1968 but the photographs themselves appeared for the first time in print 40 years ago this week. It was an image that would eventually launch a thousand environmental movements, such was its impact on the public   10
consciousness.

The three-man crew of Apollo 8 – Frank Borman, Jim Lovell and Bill Anders – were carrying out the necessary groundwork for the later manned landing on the Moon and were the first people to orbit the Moon, flying around the far side which is not visible from Earth.

They were also in effect the first people to lose complete contact with their own planet, not   15
being able to see or radio Earth for the duration of their journey behind the Moon. It was only when they completed the orbit that they could regain contact.

Ironically, for the first three orbits, the crew had their backs to the Earth as it re-appeared over the lunar horizon and did not see the iconic view that would change their lives. It was only on the fourth orbit that one of the men turned round and saw the spectacle for the   20
first time.

"Oh my God! Look at that picture over there! Isn't that something?" he said, his words captured for posterity on the on-board tape recorder. They quickly scrambled for a camera – the first couple of images of "Earthrise" were in black and white, subsequent photos were taken in colour. It is these colour photographs that became the iconic images of the environmental movement. 25

They showed the stark contrast between the grey, desolate landscape of the lifeless Moon and the vivid blue-and-white orb of the fertile Earth – a symbol of warmth and life in a bleak desert of deathly coldness.

Sir Fred Hoyle, the great British cosmologist, rightly predicted in 1948 that the first images of Earth from space would change forever our view of our own planet. "Earthrise" encapsulated the fragility of a place that seems so immense to the people who live there, but so tiny when viewed from the relatively short distance of its natural satellite. 30

And so it took catching sight of our own place in space to realise that the Earth is the only home we have, and we had better look after it. 35

Source B:

In the Clouds

Then, as we swept rapidly above the trees, I could see the roadway immediately outside the Gardens, stuck all over with rows of tiny people, looking like so many black pins on a cushion, and the hubbub of the voices below was like the sound of a distant school let loose.

And here began that peculiar panoramic effect which is the distinguishing feature of a view from a balloon, and which arises from the utter absence of all sense of motion in the machine itself. The earth appeared literally to consist of a long series of scenes, which were being continually drawn along under you, as if it were a **diorama** beheld flat upon the ground, and gave one almost the notion that the world was an endless landscape stretched upon rollers, which some invisible sprites were revolving for your especial enjoyment. 5

Then, as we struck towards the fields of Surrey, and I looked over the edge of the car in which I was standing, holding on tight to the thick rope descending from the hoop above, and with the rim of the wicker work reaching up to my breast, the sight was the most exquisite delight I ever experienced. The houses below looked like the tiny wooden things out of a child's box of toys, and the streets like ruts. To peer straight down gave you an awful sense of the height to which the balloon had already risen, and yet there was no idea of danger, for the mind was too much occupied with the grandeur and novelty of the scene all around to feel the least alarm. As the balloon kept on ascending, the lines of buildings grew smaller and smaller, till in a few minutes the projections seemed very much like the prominences on the little coloured plaster models of countries. Then we could see the gas lights along the different lines of road start into light one after another all over the earth, and presently the ground seemed to be covered with little miniature illumination lamps, such as may be seen resting on the grass at the sides of the gravel walks in suburban gardens of amusement. The river we could see winding far away, undulating, as it streamed along, like a **man-of-war's** pennant, and glittering here and there in the dusk like grey steel. All round 10 15 20 25 the horizon were thick slate-coloured clouds, edged with the orange-red of the departed sun; and with the tops of these we seemed to be on a level. So deep was the dusk in the distance, that it was difficult to tell where the earth ended and the sky began; and in trying to make out the objects afar off, it seemed to be as if you were looking through so much **crape**. The roads below were now like narrow light-brown ribbons, and the bridges across 30 the Thames almost like planks; while the tiny black barges, as they floated up the river, appeared no bigger than insects. The large green fields had dwindled down to about the size of kettle-holders, and the hedges were like strips of chenille.

Glossary:

Diorama – a scene, often in miniature, reproduced in three dimensions by placing objects, figures, etc., in front of a painted background

Man-of-war – a powerful warship from the 16th to the 19th century

Crape – a lightweight fabric with a finely crinkled or pebbled surface

Section A: Reading

Answer **all** questions in this section.

You are advised to spend about 45 minutes on this section.

| 0 | 1 | Read again the first part of **Source A**, lines 1 to 17.

Choose **four** statements below which are TRUE.

- Shade the boxes of the ones that you think are true
- Choose a maximum of four statements.

1	The astronauts had prepared to take this photograph.	⬭
2	The photograph became very well-known and influential.	⬭
3	The photograph made people realise how fragile the Earth is.	⬭
4	The astronauts were in constant contact with the Earth.	⬭
5	They were the first people to orbit the moon.	⬭
6	The astronauts called the photograph 'Earthrise'.	⬭
7	Apollo 8 was going to land on the Moon.	⬭
8	The photograph became a symbol of the Earth's importance to mankind.	⬭

[4 marks]

0 2   You need to refer to **Source A** and **Source B** for this question:

Use details from both sources. Write a summary of the differences between the things that the Apollo 8 astronauts saw and the sights seen by Henry Mayhew.

[8 marks]

0 3   You now need to refer **only** to **Source B**, Henry Mayhew's account as the balloon rises over Surrey and he looks down (from line 11 to the end).

How does Mayhew use language to make you, the reader, feel as if you're up in the balloon with him?

[12 marks]

0 4   For this question, you need to refer to the **whole of Source A** together with the **whole of Source B**.

Compare how the writers have conveyed the impact of flight and exploration on the participants.

In your answer, you could:

- compare their views and experiences
- compare the methods they use to convey those views and experiences
- support your ideas with quotations from both texts.

[16 marks]

Section B: Writing

You are advised to spend about 45 minutes on this section.

You are reminded of the need to plan your answer.

You should write in full sentences.

You should leave enough time to check your work at the end.

0 5   Space exploration is extremely expensive. We should be concentrating on ridding the world of poverty instead of wasting billions on sending rockets into space.

Write a letter to a national newspaper in which you argue for or against this view.

(24 marks for content and organization
16 marks for technical accuracy)
[40 marks]